D0043210

james bay
The plot
to drown the North Woods

by Boyce Richardson

WITHDRAWN

JUN 2 5 2020

UNBC Library

Sierra Club   San Francisco • New York
in association with
Clarke, Irwin & Company Limited
Toronto • Vancouver

UNIVERSITY OF NORTHERN
BRITISH COLUMBIA
LIBRARY
Prince George, BC

Maps by John Maroc, based on Hydro-Quebec data

Photos by Boyce Richardson

Cover photo by Bruce Litteljohn

The Sierra Club, founded in 1892 by John Muir, has devoted itself to the study
and protection of the nation's scenic and ecological resources — mountains,
wetlands, woodlands, wild shores and rivers. All Club publications are part of
the nonprofit effort the Club carries on as a public trust. There are 43 chapters
coast to coast, in Canada, Hawaii and Alaska. Participation is invited in the
Club's program to enjoy and preserve wilderness everywhere. Address: 1050
Mills Tower, San Francisco, California 94104; 373 Fifth Avenue, New York,
N.Y. 10016; 324 C Street, S. E., Washington, D.C. 2003; or Suite 18, 43 Vic-
toria Street, Toronto 1, Ontario.

Copyright © 1972 by the Sierra Club
All rights reserved
Library of Congress catalog card number 72-83982
International Standard Book number 87156-067-4

Published simultaneously in Canada by Clarke, Irwin & Company Limited
International Standard Book number 0-7720-0566-4

Printed in Canada

UNIVERSITY OF NORTHERN
BRITISH COLUMBIA
LIBRARY

Contents

Prologue

James Bay is not white man's country. Not yet. He came there early, in little ships from England. But the land was too harsh for him, the rivers too wild, the forests too dense, the distances too great. He perched precariously at the river mouths, on the great bay. He traveled inland, when the Indians would take him. But he did not leave his mark on the wilderness. Not yet.

The Cree were there before him, roaming the wilderness. The forest was their home. They moved ceaselessly over the land, hunting and trapping the animals on which they lived. When the white man came, the Cree sold him furs. But they never really came out of the bush. They remained a part of the forest.

For half of the year, the huge land lies under a long winter. The turbulent rivers freeze, and are quiet. The trees and plants await the coming of the sun. The animals forage for food, where it is exposed by the chill north winds. The Cree head into the forest, cluster in family groups, pad softly on snowshoes across the snows, watch for the signs of the animals, and kill what they need. They fear and respect nature, and love it. And when they bring down the moose they pay their respects to the Great Spirit who, they know, watches the lives of all the animals, including man.

When the sun comes, the snows melt, the rivers throw off the ice, the waters pour in great torrents to the sea. The birds arrive from the south, millions of them. The men come out of the bush to the settlements, relax, fish a little, repair their equipment, warm themselves in the northern sun, wait for the birds to pass again, flying off before the winter returns to the north.

A cold land, hostile for those who do not know it, but friendly, quiet, peaceful for those who are attuned to its rhythms, it is perhaps the last place in North America where humans depend on the animals, and the animals depend on the land.

That is how it is, still, 350 years after the first white men set foot in this northern country. The canoe and snowshoe, the hand-fashioned bush camp, the man-powered sled, the long portage overland to avoid the tumbling rapids — these remain as vital today as the imported small airplane, the rifle and the gasoline motor.

The old way is how it has always been. But not for much longer. The white man has decided, at last, to take over this last expanse of the northern woods, to tame these tempestuous and unreasonable rivers, to flood and conquer this land.

1. The World Starts Today

On April 29, 1971, in an atmosphere of frenetic partisan
political enthusiasm, the James Bay development project
was launched by the tall, thin young man, Robert
Bourassa, who a year before had been elected to the
prime ministership of the province of Quebec. It was not
only the anniversary of his accession to power, but it was
his birthday, and he gave himself quite a birthday
present as he declared to 5,000 cheering supporters of
his provincial Liberal party that his government was
committed to the largest single industrial undertaking
ever conceived in Canada — and probably in North
America.

The manner of the project's launching was no doubt
meant to be high drama, designed to display the talents
of the young premier who had occupied center stage in
the province for a year. But even at the time, the show
seemed more like tragi-comic farce, a sad commentary
on the behavior of a political-economic system that

seems now to be driving on out of the control of the people who are nominally directing it.

Bourassa had had a disastrous first year in office. His worst moments had come six months before during the kidnapping crisis, when his own senior Cabinet minister, Pierre Laporte, had been assassinated by terrorists from the Front de Libération du Québec. During this crisis, which saw the federal government impose martial law on the entire country, Bourassa had never seemed to be much more than an ineffectual messageboy for the more determined Liberal leader in Ottawa, Prime Minister Pierre Elliot Trudeau.

But now he was going to show them all that he was a strong man who could make big decisions with the best of them. He gathered his party faithful into the Coliseum in Quebec City, harangued them about the marvels of his first year in government, and then the lights were turned down while the audience was treated to an audio-visual show about the James Bay project. It was a waltz of the billions, spoken by a Quebec actor, Roland Chenail. Bourassa would dam up five, possibly seven, great rivers. He would build 60 miles of dikes, ten great dams, eleven (or more) generating stations. He would produce enough electricity to solve the energy crisis in the northeastern United States (and make Quebec rich). He would build 500 miles of roads into the north, so Canadians could get at millions of tons of iron ore. He would build airports, and a port in James Bay. Great new lakes would be created. Tourists would be able to pour in by the thousands. He would spend $400 million in electrical equipment and machinery, $335 million in cement, $320 million in pylons. And would he ever create electricity — 10 million kilowatts, 100 billion kilowatt - hours every year. Seventy million cubic yards of earth would be moved, 20 million cubic yards of rock blasted.

He would spend $6 billion, if he spent a penny. And jobs! He would create 125,000 jobs for unemployed Quebecers. The James Bay project was big, but big!

"The world begins today," exclaimed Mr. Chenail, as pictures of rockets, missiles, jet planes, turbines and the like flashed across the screen. Bourassa then rose (modestly, no doubt) and announced that he had received a letter from Roland Giroux, president of Hydro-Quebec, the province's publicly owned power utility, which had been studying the feasibility of the scheme since 1964. Giroux had written: "Hydro-Quebec recommends to the government of Quebec that the project for the hydro-electric development of James Bay be undertaken without delay."

"We are proud to say," cried Bourassa, "that we agree with Hydro-Quebec. The development of James Bay is a project without precedent in the economic history of Quebec. It is a turning point in our history.

"James Bay is the key to the economic and social progress of Quebec, the key to the political stability of Quebec, the key to the future of Quebec." Only such a project could break the vicious circle of the economic depression in the province, could respond to the anguish of the thousands of young people arriving on the labor market, could involve the collectivity of Quebecers in the development of the province's natural resources. "It will no longer be said that we live poorly on such a rich land," said Bourassa. "We will get out of our situation of economic inferiority."

Exceptionally for such a huge announcement, so pregnant with questions and detail, Bourassa did not make any background material available to the press, nor did he hold a press conference at which he could be questioned. Instead, bewildered journalists found themselves groping in the dark of the Coliseum as the audio-visual show boomed on, trying vainly to scribble a few notes about the glories to come — notes on which they had to base their stories for the next day, Saturday. Bourassa had carefully given interviews beforehand to the state-owned television channel. He had the whole weekend, as it were, to hog the headlines. And, in a manner of speaking, it worked. The James Bay project was launched as if it were likely to save not only Bourassa's job and the electoral prospects of the Liberal party but Quebec itself, even the Canadian confederation. He made it sound, as one political commentator remarked sourly, like the biggest thing since the pyramids.

It is impossible to separate the James Bay project from the manner in which it was launched. Probably no other project of similar scale has ever been put on foot for such nakedly political purposes, and with so little attempt to disguise those political purposes. Bourassa had been elected to power a year before on a promise that he would create 100,000 jobs for Quebecers. He did not know how this was to be done, but because he was an economist, presumably he would be able to think of something. Bourassa's rise to power had been startling. He had been his party's economic spokesman in the Quebec National Assembly during several years in opposition. It was only at the beginning of 1970 when the old party leader, former provincial Prime Minister Jean Lesage, was forced to give up his office that Bourassa came from nowhere to win the job after a costly leadership campaign. His success was not unconnected with the fact that he had married into one of Quebec's wealthiest families. He had its money and influence behind him, and the whole Quebec establishment — especially the economically dominant, English-speaking establishment — had rallied round him and forced him into the leadership. A few months later he swept the province in a provincial election. The former governing party, the Union Nationale, was practically annihilated but the rising separatist party, the Parti Québecois, won a quarter of the votes. Bourassa's election enabled federalists to breathe easily. For some years Quebec had been in a state of turmoil as feeling for an independent sovereign state gained ground, particularly among the young. Following the triumph of Expo 67, the province had entered a disastrous economic slump. The neighboring province of Ontario raced ahead in investment and wealth, while potential investors were scared away by the apparent political instability of Quebec.

When Bourassa took office he must indeed have dreamed of recreating some of the excitement and élan that had accompanied the Quiet Revolution ushered in by Lesage in the first years of the sixties. It was the Lesage government — indeed, it was mainly René Lévesque, the man who later quit the Liberals to become the separatist leader — which had nationalized the private electricity-generating companies and created in Hydro-Quebec the one incontestably successful, large, commercial enterprise conceived, designed and run by French Canadians. Hydro-Quebec had in those heady years captured the imagination of younger Quebecers with its bold schemes. The huge dam at Manicouagan, in the northeastern interior of the province, had become a symbol of the Quebec resurgence, and Georges Dor, one of many excellent Quebec singers, had turned it into an element of popular culture with his famous song, "La Manic."

Bourassa had to create jobs and enthusiasm. And if it had worked once, why should it not work again? If Lesage and Levesque could capture the enthusiasm of the nation with a dam, why couldn't he do the same?

Only with ten dams? In his search for projects that
would create jobs, Bourassa dusted off abandoned
schemes that were mouldering in the files. One of them,
a proposal for an east-west auto route through Montreal,
had been designed fifteen years before. But he pushed it
through against the wishes of the city, the metropolitan
government and the citizens. The other file that he took
down was the abandoned scheme for the James Bay
project. Within fifteen days of taking office, he set up a
committee composed of officials from several government departments and of representatives of Hydro-
Quebec to study the proposal to harness the electricity
potential of the rivers running into James Bay. It had
been studied first in 1964, perfunctorily, and then in
detail in 1967. Both reports had been negative. But that
meant nothing to Bourassa. As soon as he got into office
he began twisting Hydro-Quebec's arm. In 1967, as
Lionel Cahill, director-general of engineering for Hydro-
Quebec, later reported, the utility had decided that
rather than develop James Bay power "it appeared
preferable to add around 1978 one or more thermal or
nuclear power stations near the main consumption centers." Never mind that. Bourassa had created expectations of some economic miracle that would save the
province from stagnation and beat off the separatist
threat. And he was determined. Hydro-Quebec swung
into action with more field studies on James Bay during
the summer of 1970, while Bourassa went off around the
world — New York, Paris, London — to try to get some
of the world's wealthiest financiers to invest in his province. Ironically, he was in New York in October, 1970,
trying to drum up this foreign money at the very moment
that the Front de Libération du Québec (FLQ) struck
and denounced Quebec governments for their sub-
servience to foreign capitalism. It was in New York, on

that same trip, that Bourassa told the Canadian Society about his James Bay dreams, about the project that would cost "a staggering $2 billion." And he added: "With the shortage of fuel, coal, oil and gas, Quebec feels it can have a major role to play in solving the northeast United States' energy problem."

That "staggering $2 billion" just kept going up, until sixteen or seventeen months later even Bourassa himself was refusing to deny that the eventual cost might be $10 billion. But by then of course he had long since made the decision to go ahead, though it soon became clear that the necessary studies to establish the cost of the power had not been done. Bourassa returned from New York to find that his province, and indeed the whole country, had been thrown into a turmoil by the FLQ kidnappers. Until December, when the crisis was finally resolved, he had little time to think of anything else. It is beyond the purview of this book to establish how the crisis damaged Bourassa's political position. But of all the leading figures, it was Bourassa who came out of the crisis worst: he had appeared indecisive, pliable and scared, and had created a crisis of conscience in his province by tamely inviting the federal government to activate the War Measures Act under the guise of an "apprehended insurrection." While some federal ministers raved on about an armed force of 3,000 terrorists waiting to destroy civilized society (it now appears that the total number of committed terrorists was more like three dozen), Bourassa was the man who could have stopped the escalation. He did not do so, and by December he was more in need of a political life line than ever. James Bay moved higher in his priorities. It would, after all, make a splash. And did he need a splash.

Hydro-Quebec pursued its studies of the James Bay project in a measured way, and during October Robert

Boyd, one of the directors, told the press that the project
would cost between $2.5 billion and $3 billion. This was,
of course, for a scheme to divert the Nottaway and
Broadback rivers through a series of canals into the
Rupert River, and to build some generating stations on
that river. This was the only scheme of which serious
studies had ever been made. It appears, however, that
Bourassa was unhappy with this measured pace. He is
said to have "strongly suggested" to Hydro-Quebec that
it hire two firms of consulting engineers to study the best
means of realizing the project.[1] These two firms were
given their mandate by Hydro-Quebec on November 10,
1970. It is obvious from their terms of reference that
some of the requirements were political, and had nothing
to do with electrical production. They were to acquaint
themselves with the Hydro-Quebec studies up to that
time, "to advise the commission as soon as possible so as
to establish a general practical and economical concept
for the development of the hydroelectric potential of the
region," and to "indicate briefly the economic benefits
which would ensue to the province in the construction
and manufacturing industries and in various other
fields." Included in their mandate was that they examine
the possibility the scheme could be carried out in stages
"so as to allow the construction to be suspended for
varying lengths of time dependent on the economic
situation." Additionally, they were to see whether certain
preliminary works such as roads, bridges, airports,
camps and forest clearings could begin as early as
possible and "so improve the Quebec employment
situation."

The firms, in other words, were asked to discover the
economic marvels that would accrue to Quebec from the
James Bay development, and to produce their reports
before March 1, 1971 — less than four months! They

went to work with a will (as which firm faced with the dazzling prospect of millions of dollars of work for the next decade would not?) and, sure enough, they found that economic marvels could be produced. Their reports arrived on March 10, 1971. Asselin, Benoit, Boucher, Ducharme and Lapointe, a Montreal firm, suggested that 12,094 megawatts could be developed for $7 billion, and would create 138,000 jobs — just what Bourassa wanted to hear. If the program were hurried along, the province could have a block of 2,000 megawatts of power available for export for ten years, beginning in 1976. Rousseau, Sauvé, Warren and Associates, which is a Quebec branch of the powerful Toronto consulting firm of Acres Ltd., suggested that 15,400 megawatts could be developed eventually for $7 billion. Hydro-Quebec, in a preliminary report, suggested that the Nottaway-Broadback-Rupert complex could develop 5,300 megawatts of capacity for $3.5 billion. The two private firms included estimates for developing the power potential of two large rivers farther north, the La Grande and the Eastmain. One of the schemes even suggested that two still more northerly rivers, the Caniapiscau, which flows north into Ungava Bay, and La Grande Baleine (Great Whale River), which flows into Hudson Bay, be diverted into the scheme. Between them all, they were suggesting modifications in drainage basins amounting to more than 170,000 square miles — an area one-quarter the size of Quebec Province, and considerably bigger than the United Kingdom.

These convenient conclusions were just what Bourassa was wanting to hear. Within six weeks of receipt of the reports he was on his feet before his loyal Liberal party supporters announcing the biggest scheme in the history of Quebec Province. No one in any way connected with the project had expected so precipitate a decision. The

ministerial committee that Bourassa had himself created
within fifteen days of assuming office was engaged in a
plan of work leading up to a report in September, 1971.
It proposed this plan to the Cabinet only two weeks
before Bourassa announced the decision to go
ahead — a decision which some members of this committee read about with astonishment in the newspapers.
L'Office de développement et de planification du
Québec (the nearest thing Quebec has to an economic
planning board), not long before Bourassa made his
decision, poured cold water on the James Bay scheme in
a report on development in northwest Quebec. It said the
James Bay project was only in the stage of preliminary
study. Work could not begin before 1976 because before
launching an enterprise which would require in-
vestments of $3 billion it would be necessary to spend 0.5
percent in studies designed to establish its feasibility. If
this were not done "one would risk that solutions might
be adopted which would cause considerable superfluous
costs." The same report doubted that a new hydro
capacity in northwest Quebec would be more useful for
Quebec than thermal or nuclear plants.

Hydro-Quebec had a plan of technical work which
would have cost $5 million for technical studies during
the summer of 1971, and it would produce a report the
following September. This was stated by Roland Giroux
in his annual report, tabled two weeks after Bourassa announced the scheme was to proceed. In the event,
Bourassa gave Hydro-Quebec $28 million for field
studies in 1971, and told it to get on with the job. There
is no evidence that Hydro-Quebec was within even a year
of being ready to pronounce on the economic viability of
the Nottaway-Broadback-Rupert project. And no one
had done serious studies of any kind concerning the

Eastmain and La Grande rivers when Bourassa announced that they would be harnessed.

Thus the decision was taken before the scheme's economic viability was established. And that was not all: only passing acknowledgment was made of the fact that all the land in question was already occupied and used by Indians. And no prior heed of any kind had been paid to the environmental consequences of such large-scale intervention in natural systems. Jabbed along by his senior advisor and father figure, Paul Desrochers, Bourassa made the big decision long, long before anyone had given any thought to the real implications of the project.

But no one could accuse him of timidity now.

Notes For Chapter I:
1. This sequence of events has been drawn together from many sources. *Québec-Presse*, the only newspaper which has taken a consistent interest in the James Bay project, first revealed most of this information, and its sources have proved consistently accurate.

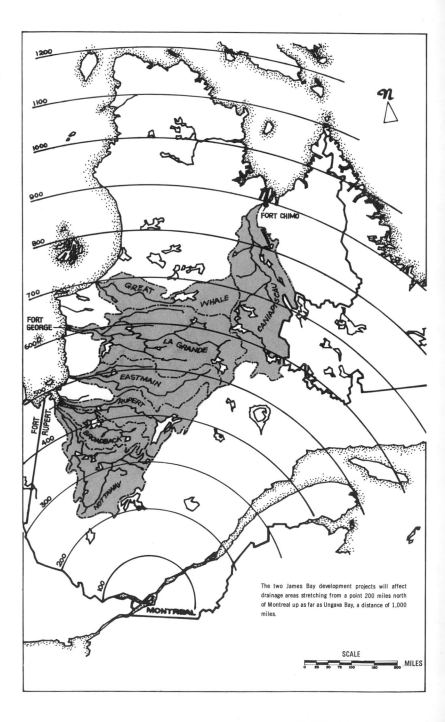

The two James Bay development projects will affect drainage areas stretching from a point 200 miles north of Montreal up as far as Ungava Bay, a distance of 1,000 miles.

SCALE

0 25 50 75 100 150 200 MILES

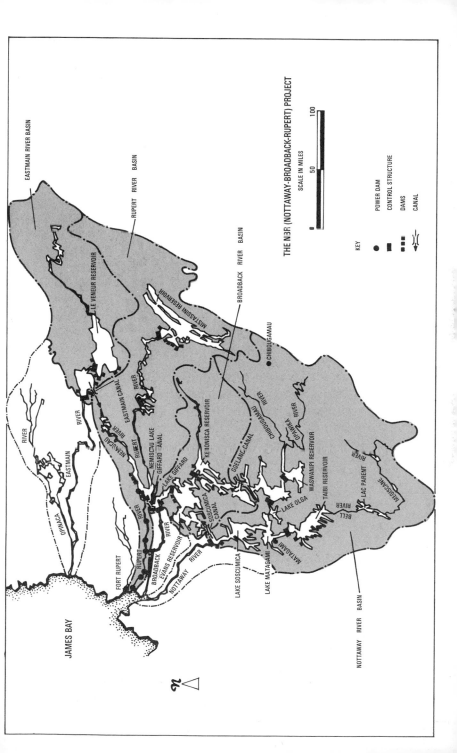

THE N3R (NOTTAWAY-BROADBACK-RUPERT) PROJECT

SCALE IN MILES

KEY

● POWER DAM
■ CONTROL STRUCTURE
┇ DAMS
↓ CANAL

EASTMAIN RIVER BASIN

RUPERT RIVER BASIN

BROADBACK RIVER BASIN

NOTTAWAY RIVER BASIN

JAMES BAY

LE VENEUR RESERVOIR

MISTASSINI RESERVOIR

EASTMAIN CANAL

NEMISCAU LAKE
GIFFARD CANAL

LAKE GIFFARD

KE IONISCA RESERVOIR

GUELANE CANAL

CHIBOUGAMAU
RIVER

OPAWIKA RIVER

WASWANIPI RESERVOIR

LAKE OLGA

TAIBI RESERVOIR

LAC PARENT

MEGISCANE RIVER

BELL RIVER

SOSCUMICA CANAL

LAKE SOSCUMICA

LAKE MATAGAMI

MATAGAMI

EVANS RESERVOIR

NOTTAWAY RIVER

BROADBACK RIVER

RUPERT RIVER

FORT RUPERT

EASTMAIN RIVER

OPINACA RIVER

NEMISCAU RIVER

RUPERT RIVER

CHIBOUGAMAU

N

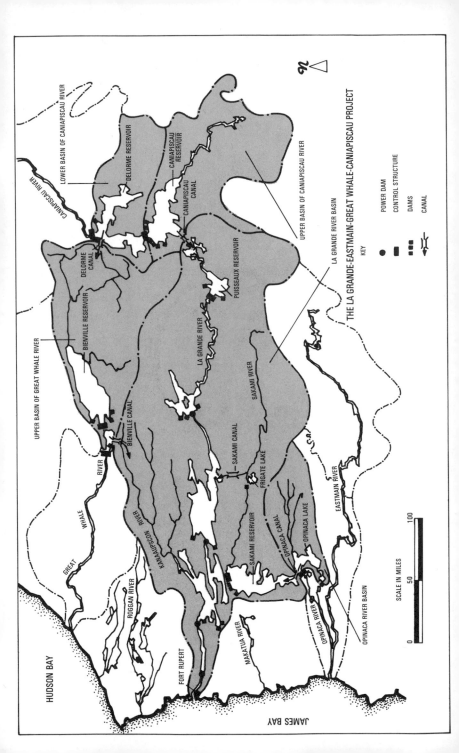

THE LA GRANDE-EASTMAIN-GREAT WHALE-CANIAPISCAU PROJECT

KEY

● POWER DAM
■ CONTROL STRUCTURE
▪▪▪ DAMS
⇥ CANAL

SCALE IN MILES

0   50   100

HUDSON BAY

JAMES BAY

CANIAPISCAU RIVER

LOWER BASIN OF CANIAPISCAU RIVER

DELORME RESERVOIR

CANIAPISCAU RESERVOIR

CANIAPISCAU CANAL

DELORME CANAL

BIENVILLE RESERVOIR

PUISSEAUX RESERVOIR

UPPER BASIN OF CANIAPISCAU RIVER

LA GRANDE RIVER BASIN

UPPER BASIN OF GREAT WHALE RIVER

LA GRANDE RIVER

BIENVILLE CANAL

SAKAMI RIVER

SAKAMI CANAL

FRIGATE LAKE

SAKAMI RESERVOIR

OPINACA CANAL

OPINACA LAKE

EASTMAIN RIVER

OPINACA RIVER

OPINACA RIVER BASIN

GREAT WHALE RIVER

ROGGAN RIVER

KANAAUPSCOW RIVER

MAKATUA RIVER

FORT RUPERT

2. A Virgin Land

The huge area in which Bourassa dreams of diverting great rivers, creating great lakes and building plants and factories, is the most significant remaining wilderness of eastern Canada — and therefore of the eastern part of the North American continent. It is about as far north from Montreal as Maine is from New York. But in Canada, whose people live along a 100-mile strip stretched over 4,000 miles of the continent, anything as far north as that is practically unknown country. The Canadian north is one of the biggest wilderness areas left in the world. It contains thousands of lakes, hundreds of large rivers, and in its nearer reaches is heavily forested. Far to the north above the tree line, lies the world's greatest cold desert. It is hard to say how Canadians regard this immense hinterland, for few of them know it. But its presence in the Canadian mind seems to take two forms. The most common of these was summed up by former Prime Minister John Diefenbaker when he discovered his "vision of the north," of a great land, full of riches, just waiting to be developed, a country lying in wait for the eager pioneers to fill it and tame' it, offering opportunity fit to bedazzle the eyes of any civilized nation. It is this "vision" which on the whole lies behind the Canadian government's attitude to the north, for the priority is definitely on "developing" this great land, on exploiting its natural riches and taming its savage moods.

The other form that the north assumes in the Canadian mind is a more gentle one, and exists for those people who know it well. For though its climate is harsh, its summer brief, its winters interminable and its isolation intense, it exerts a fascination which touches almost everyone who ventures into it. The scale of this vast empty country cannot be matched — at least anywhere else in the western world. For a city man to fly north into this country is a challenge to most of his assumptions because it seems to go on endlessly, and man, where he has tried, has made only feeble scratches on its surface. Awe inspiring, too, apart from its immensity, is its beauty, its wide range of colors, the vivacity and temper of its moods. Is there anything in the world comparable to the purity of one of those days in northern Canada, utterly still, when the temperature drops to forty and fifty below zero, and all of life seems to have been etched by some master craftsman on a three-dimensional plate of sharp, brittle air? This great wilderness is occupied, especially in its more southerly forested parts, by Indians who have dealt with its harsh moods for untold generations, people who know their way by foot over most of its territory, to whom the indistinguishable maze of lakes and rivers and forests is as familiar as the back of their own hands. These people live close to the animals in this great land, and their world-view is dominated by that relationship.

Yet it is only in comparatively recent years, as the

developers have driven north, that Canadians as a whole have begun to understand that this great north of theirs, seemingly bountiful and empty, is really a delicately balanced system of life forces, each interacting with the other in a balance which can be destroyed by a single careless act. The environmental movement of recent years has forced the Canadian government to bring in regulations demanding high standards of environmental care of anyone who wants to change the landscape, use the waters, or dig up and transport the minerals. The problem is not so intense in the nearer wilderness, which is better watered, heavily forested and less fragile than the tundra in the far north. But here, too, the white man from the south has imported an exploitative mentality. This forest land is known and properly understood in its totality by only one group of people, the Indians, who respect its subtle and complex relationships. The white man, on the whole, has concentrated on clearcutting huge squares of the little trees (which take up to 125 years to grow to any sort of size) and hacking and digging into the earth with little consideration for the effects of his actions.

Most of all the white man has shown little regard for the effect of his presence on the Indians. Almost everywhere the white man has moved with his bulldozers into the boreal forest, he has simply pushed the Indians aside and invaded their trap lines and hunting grounds without so much as a by-your-leave. Only in Alberta and British Columbia, the westernmost provinces, have any sizable populations moved into these northern lands. In most other provinces mere fingers of development — almost always attached to mineral ore bodies — have shot out into the wilderness. Small towns have been created around these mines and mills. The towns are the colonial outposts of a commercial empire

In Matthew Neeposh's hunting camp north of Mistassini, the roof, and firewood pile up by the door, are picked out by snow. The hunter's snowshoes, shovel and sled are hand-made.

A typical view of the terrain in the James Bay project area.

whose decisions are made elsewhere and are designed to benefit other people in other places. Many of these northern towns are among the worst in the country. They are dominated by the companies that run the mines or mills, whose executives stay in the area only for an average of three or four years before moving on to better jobs in the cities. The pollution from the town's meal ticket is often bad, and the distinguishing feature of these towns is the poverty, grime and squalor which are allowed to exist despite the wealth the workers create through their labor.

The experience of Quebec in taming its north has not been a happy one. In effect only two parts of Quebec's north have been at all developed. One of them is the iron-ore-producing district inland near the Labrador border, where small company towns devote themselves to digging the riches out of the ground and sending it off — at bargain-basement prices — to Pittsburgh. The other is the Abitibi region, directly south of James Bay. During the depression this was the object of Quebec's quaintly but accurately named Colonization Department. Unemployed workers were sent north, given some poor land, and told to be farmers. It is a poignant experience today to drive around the back roads of the Abitibi region past the hundreds of abandoned frame shacks these poor colonists tried to call home. The pathetic squares of land that they hacked out of the bush are gradually being reclaimed by the bush. And not only has the Abitibi agriculture collapsed: the mines are closing too. Some 40 percent of the people in the area are on welfare. Now they hear that the experience is to be repeated, the leap north is to take place over their heads, the men in the south have their eyes on still more distant riches for extraction.

Despite being relatively unknown, the part of this

great Canadian northland east of James Bay has played
an important part in Canadian history, and has always
harbored a style of life as distinctive as the wilderness itself.

This land emerged from the retreating ice cap only
8,000 to 9,000 years ago, and the ice was replaced by the
Tyrell Sea, which covered the low-lying coastal areas
along James Bay until about 5,000 years ago.[1] The relief
from the weight of the ice caused an "upwarping" of the
land and its emergence from the sea. Some archaeologists believe that human beings have been in the
inland areas since between 5,000 and 4,000 B.C., and
that the present-day Cree can be traced back to these
prehistoric inhabitants. The archaeologists assume,
from having discovered paleo-Indian specimens in the
northern tundra areas, that others are hidden under
forest cover farther south. But certainly artifacts have
been discovered indicating human habitation from
about 3,000 B.C., associated with stone tools, moving into a pottery stage at a later period. The archaeologists
date the Cree from before A.D. 1,000, and they were certainly there when Henry Hudson sailed into James Bay in
1611. Hudson believed he had found the passage to the
east that all the English explorers of the time were after,
and he kept his men sailing south until they reached the
Bottom of the Bay, and were becalmed there. They
managed to live through the winter, losing only one man
to scurvy. But the voyage home was hardly begun before
some of Hudson's crew mutinied and put the captain, his
son and some of the feebler sailors adrift in an open
boat, after which they were never heard of again. (When
I visited the east coast of Hudson Bay during the summer
of 1971 and talked to old Eskimo hunters, I heard vague
tales from them of word having been handed down orally
about three strangers whom their forebears had

discovered in the bay many years before, and murdered.)

It was in the James Bay area that the famous Hudson's Bay Company, which now operates large department stores in most Canadian cities and a string of tiny trading posts in settlements throughout the Canadian north, got its start. The French adventurers Pierre Esprit Radisson and his brother-in-law Médard Chouart, Sieur des Groseilliers, disappeared into the northern bush one year and are believed by some authorities — although it is unproven — to have crossed the Canadian shield from Lake Superior to James Bay during a trading trip by canoe. They were punished by the French authorities, and took a piquant revenge — a year or two later they visited England where they found patrons to outfit two ships for a journey to Hudson Bay in 1668. The *Nonsuch*, with Groseilliers aboard, completed the voyage, wintered in Rupert Bay at the bottom of James Bay, and returned in 1669 with a profitable cargo of furs. Today in Rupert House, a settlement which might well be destroyed by the diverted waters of the James Bay project, a plaque declares that the town was founded by Groseilliers in 1668. It was in 1670 that the Royal Charter was granted to "the Governor and Company of Adventurers trading into Hudson's Bay," by which they became Lords and Proprietors of all territories accessible by Hudson Strait that were not already subject to another Christian state. They were empowered to appoint magistrates, make civil and criminal laws, and enforce a penal code. Charles Fort was set up on Rupert River. When the news was received in Quebec, the French authorities sent a Jesuit priest, Father Charles Albanel, to James Bay to investigate. True to his evangelizing mission, he urged the Indians "to shun the Europeans who are trading towards the North Sea," because among these people "prayer is not offered to

God." Better by far that they should carry their furs to
Fort St. John "where you will find some black gown to
instruct and to baptise."

The struggle between the French and English traders
working out of James Bay is one of the most colorful and
bizarre in North American history. The Hudson's Bay
Company men sat in their forts at the Bottom of the Bay,
as they called it, for nearly 100 years, trading with the
Indians who came down the rivers to their posts. The
company men were timid and reluctant to venture into
the interior. But the Frenchmen from Montreal, the
remarkable *coureurs de bois*, made incredible canoe
journeys through the interior, married the Indian
women, spoke the Indian languages, and tried to cut off
the supply of furs to the English along the rivers.
Radisson and Groseilliers kept changing sides: in 1684
Radisson captured a fort on the bay for the English
(taking his own nephew prisoner in the process), which
he had built for the French the year before. In 1686
James Bay was the scene of "one of the most successful
commando raids in the history of North American war-
fare" when a force of 100 men, led by Pierre de Troyes,
son of a Paris attorney and a former captain in the
French army, made an extraordinary three-month
overland journey to James Bay, and there captured the
three posts of Rupert House, Fort Albany and Moose
Factory, with hardly any resistance from their somewhat
undisciplined and unwary English occupants.[2]

Through all of these years James Bay had more contact with Europe, directly, than with the French settlements along the St. Lawrence. It has remained until
fairly recently one of the most remote areas in North
America. Its particularity has continued until our own
day: isolated, yet full of life, an area in which human,
animal and plant life has lived on its own terms, never

too much bothered by outside influences. The Hudson's Bay Company traders were supplied by the once-yearly ship that arrived at the Bottom of the Bay during the two-and-a-half-month, ice-free navigation season, with a year's supply of goods. That was the traders' line of communication, and right into this century, they had more to do with England than with Canada, and practically nothing at all with Quebec. They ran their region from Rupert House. Powered by Indian canoe men, they carried their goods up the wild rivers that are now to be diverted and tamed, to the inland posts, and brought the furs down in return after the trapping season. The headwaters of the rivers that run into James Bay are separated by a thousand miles, far off in western Ontario and in eastern Quebec. These rivers were the highways for the Indians. "They are among the most turbulent and unreasonable rivers in the world," according to Professor Kenneth Hare, a leading climatologist of Hudson Bay. Glen Speers, manager of the Hudson's Bay Company post at Mistassini, who has spent most of his life in the tiny settlements and has been up and down the rivers by canoe many times, says: "There are more beautiful rivers in a small area here than anywhere else in the world."

These wild rivers lie quiet most of the year. But in the spring when the waters thaw and the snow which covers all the land in their great basins melts, they rush to the sea in a gigantic flood. Consider the three southern rivers, which under the Bourassa scheme will all flow to the sea through one channel. The Nottaway, which was flowing at only 9,000 cubic feet a second (cfs) at the beginning of April, 1962, was up to 116,000 cfs only two months later, and then quickly diminished. The Broadback in the same year rushed from 3,500 cfs to 26,000. And the Rupert, whose minimum flow was down to

13,000 cfs halfway through April, six weeks later had quadrupled its flow. Between the three of them, their flow increased from 25,500 cfs to nearly 200,000, a rush of water which swept out into James Bay and aided enormously in breaking up the ice there.

Nature, of course, has provided a complex regime of aquatic and terrestrial fauna and flora which has adjusted to these wild fluctuations. Until now men have been able to live in the region only by paying their respects to the wild nature which surrounds them. The ones who know this country best, the Indians, have made a religion of respecting its other forms of life. The wildness and difficulty of the rivers has never stopped the Indians from wandering the country and they have developed a modest appreciation of their own role in this delicate system. The canoe in summer, the snowshoe in winter, are still their means of locomotion. Beaver, moose, caribou, otter, mink, rabbit and fish abound. Geese and ducks arrive in James Bay by the million every spring and autumn. They are the companions whose presence or absence dictates the annual rhythm of the Indian life.

The white man has been in the area since his early days in North America. But so far he has never really set his imprint on it — a triumph of nature, if ever there was one.

But now all that is to change. The wilderness cannot be left alone to perform its necessary function of carrying and reviving that life on which we all depend on this earth. Now the white man can make his presence felt. His airplanes can take him there, complete with his imported climate and gigantic earthmoving machines. He needs the power that those wild rivers can provide. The rapids are to disappear: the portages of five and six miles will no longer be laboriously hauled by the Indians; the tempestuous floods will be flattened out to the engineer's "estimated regulated flow." And if the white man really succeeds as he hopes to do, open-pit mines will gouge the land and factories and processing plants will belch smoke into the pure, cold air. Progress will have arrived by 1982. And the last great wilderness of the eastern continent will be tamed.

Notes For Chapter II:
1. For an account of the history and prehistory of the area, see the first two chapters in *Science, History and Hudson Bay, Volume 1*, published by the Department of Energy, Mines and Resources, Ottawa.
2. A detailed account of this remarkable journey is given in *The Battle for James Bay, 1686*, by W.A. Kenyon and J.R. Turnbull, Macmillan of Canada.

3. Taming The Great North

If Bourassa's object was to show the world that he could think up as big a scheme as anyone else, he certainly succeeded in that. The James Bay project is on a colossal scale and involves an intervention in natural systems which would immediately be recognized as unacceptable if anybody other than a small number of Indians were living in the territory. Involved are five, and possibly seven, large rivers flowing across Quebec from the south and east into James, Hudson and Ungava bays (not to mention at least nine major tributaries whose waters will also be affected). The headwaters are located in country from 800 to 1,200 feet above sea level, mostly between 400 and 500 miles from the coast. The land is unaccented, and the rivers run through a network of lakes until about 100 miles from the coast, where the land begins to drop from about 750 feet toward sea level. The southern point of James Bay — Rupert Bay, into which the three southernmost rivers flow — is about 450 miles from Montreal. The project area extends 250 miles north along the James Bay coast, and inland approximately 300 miles.

The scheme essentially consists of two parts. One is to harness the three southern rivers (the Nottaway, Broadback and Rupert) by blocking off the Nottaway and Broadback, diverting their waters through a system of lakes and canals into the Rupert and building a number of power stations in a ladder along that river. This is called the NBR project, and until 1970 it was the only project for James Bay development that had been given any serious consideration.

The second part involves harnessing the main northern rivers, La Grande, the Great Whale, the Caniapiscau, and also the Opinaca, a tributary of the Eastmain, and diverting huge additional quantities of water into the La Grande channel, through four generating stations scattered among the nine great reservoirs that would be created. It is this scheme, the Quebec government announced in May, 1972, which is to proceed first.

If all these schemes are put into operation, the watershed affected will, at its closest point, be 200 miles north of Montreal, and at its farthest, in Ungava Bay, nearly 1,000 miles north. The total area to be modified would vary, according to different estimates, between 144,000 and 174,000 square miles. Such a scheme would span a wide variety of wilderness country, from the sensitive clays of the southern part through wide expanses of swamp and forest and through the tree line to the northern tundra. The average annual temperature ranges from about 32° F. in the south to 25° F. in the north, and precipitation, of which about a third is snow, from forty inches a year in the south to twenty-five in the north. The extent of the interventions in the natural system can be gauged from the profiles of the rivers.

The *Rupert* rises in Lake Mistassini, the biggest freshwater lake in Quebec, and runs 320 miles down to the sea at Rupert Bay. It drains an area of 16,700 square miles, and drops 680 feet in the last 60 miles of its length (only 10 feet a mile). Its recorded flow varies between a minimum of 11,000 cubic feet per second (cfs) to a maximum of 65,000 cfs. The first stage of the proposed scheme (after the construction of roads, airports and communication networks) would divert the waters of the Rupert temporarily into the Broadback through tunnels to permit construction of four generating stations on that river. The second stage would be to turn Nemiscau Lake (elevation 755 feet) and Mistassini Lake (elevation 1,230 feet) into reservoirs by building a system of dikes. This would raise the level of Nemiscau Lake by 30 feet, extending its area from 80 to 160 square miles, and raise Mistassini Lake by 40 feet, extending its area from 925 to 1,390 square miles. It would flood half the Indian villages on the lakes' shores in the process. The same tunnels would later be used to divert the Nottaway and Broadback into the Rupert.

The *Broadback* is the smallest of the major rivers involved. It flows 300 miles, drains 8,400 square miles, drops 680 feet in its final 75 miles, and has been known to vary in flow from 2,600 cfs at its low point to 30,000 cfs at its maximum. This river would be blocked off about 83.5 miles from the coast, and its waters diverted into the Rupert. The lower reaches of the river, therefore, would carry only the tiny amounts of runoff that flow into it during its final 83 miles. Two reservoirs would be created on the Broadback from small existing lakes. They would be the Giffard, whose level would be raised 32 feet and area extended from a mere 35 to 139 square miles (more than quadrupling its size), and the Evans, whose level would be raised 38 feet and area extended from 270 to 510 square miles.

The *Nottaway* rises nearly 1,400 feet above sea level at

a point 460 miles from the sea, drains 25,000 square miles, drops 800 feet in its final 110 miles, and has been known to vary in flow from a minimum of 7,800 cfs to a maximum of 116,000. It runs through numerous little lakes, and has many tributaries. The third phase of the project would be to build a long canal to carry the Nottaway waters into the Broadback reservoirs (and so into the Rupert). The Nottaway too would be blocked off 92 miles from the sea. The last phase of the project would be to develop an extensive system of reservoirs in the southern parts of the area to control the Nottaway system. These reservoirs would be the Taibi, whose level would be raised 36 feet, and area extended from 37 to a whopping 330 square miles (an expansion of nine times); the Goeland and Waswanipi reservoirs, which would be raised 50 and 35 feet and extended in area from 220 to 435 square miles; and the Soscumica and Matagami lakes, which would be raised 32 and 17 feet and extended in area from 153 to 432 square miles. In all, the NBR scheme would completely block off two great rivers and extend nine lakes which now measure 1,709 square miles into reservoirs of roughly twice the size.

The decision on whether to proceed with damming these rivers will be made in five years.

The northern project involves even bigger areas:

The *La Grande* (formerly Fort George) River rises 460 miles from the sea at 1,650 feet elevation, drains an area of 37,400 square miles, has been known to vary in flow from a minimum of 11,800 cfs to a maximum of 208,000 cfs. Eight reservoirs will be built on and around this river, raising levels as much as 450 feet and expanding the water surface by four times. The Great Whale River to the north and the Caniapiscau, whose headwaters lie to the east will be blocked. Both of these rivers run through tundra. The Great Whale will provide a big reservoir of 420 square miles from which water will be diverted to the La Grande system through a canal; and two reservoirs will be formed on the Caniapiscau, totaling 1,290 square miles (compared with 385 square miles at present). From the south the Opinaca River, a tributary of the Eastmain, will also be blocked off, and its waters diverted into the La Grande. These proposals will reduce the flow of the lower reaches of the Eastmain by 30 percent, of the 230 downstream miles of the Great Whale River by 50 percent, and of the Caniapiscau by 40 percent.

Between the NBR and the La Grande lies the 450-mile long *Eastmain*, draining 18,300 square miles, dropping 600 feet in its final 75 miles, varying between a high flow of 122,000 cfs and a minimum of 5,100 cfs, and according to one engineer's report, capable of being so developed that six generating stations could provide 2,100 megawatts of electricity. Three reservoirs would have to be built.

This was the scheme, in outline, as announced by Bourassa on April 29, 1971. It has since been admitted that the two northern rivers, the Eastmain and the La Grande, were thrown in by the prime minister in an excess of enthusiasm, apparently to make the scheme sound even more impressive than it really was. No detailed technical work had been done in the field at these two rivers; Bourassa had at hand nothing but the quickie reports so obligingly produced by the two firms of consulting engineers hired by Hydro-Quebec the previous November. These hardly pretend to be satisfactory engineering studies — one of them refers to engineers having made only three trips to the area. But such details did not worry the young prime minister. He added the two northern rivers anyway, and elevated the cost from $3.5 billion, which Hydro-Quebec had settled on as likely for the NBR project, to $6 billion — a nice round figure.

The escalation had been impressive; the conversion had taken place like lightning — for only six months before Bourassa had told the press that in the present economic conditions the government could not afford to invest $2 billion in the James Bay project. Six months later: $6 billion. And a year after that: maybe $10 billion.

There has never been a dance of the billions to equal it, at least in the history of Canada. And even though almost every conceivable question — about cost, economic effects, the environment or the Indians — remained unanswered, the young prime minister pressed on. The summer was occupied in a vicious Parliamentary battle, as the separatist Parti Québecois fought to stall Bill 50 setting up the James Bay Development Corporation (in French, Société de Développement de la Baie James). If the prospect of a huge energy sellout to the United States infuriated *Canadian* nationalists, the decision not to entrust the project to Hydro-Quebec infuriated Quebec nationalists. The expansion of Hydro-Quebec through nationalization of private power companies had been, symbolically, one of the most important events in recent Quebec history. It was perhaps because Hydro-Quebec had already become so powerful that Bourassa did not want to increase its power by entrusting it with the huge project. So the new corporation was set up and given $10 million and nearly dictatorial powers over the huge territory, with a mandate to "promote the development and exploitation of the area." This enormous area was declared a municipality — because it is about the size of England, it surely must be the biggest municipality in the

world — and the five directors were declared members
of the municipal council. Bourassa named Pierre
Nadeau, the relatively obscure vice-president of the Industrial Acceptance Corporation, to the presidency of the
James Bay Corporation (after some more prominent
Quebecers had refused the office). The corporation also
has a full-time vice-president and three part-time directors, including the president of Hydro-Quebec. That
Hydro-Quebec and the prime minister did not see eye to
eye on the James Bay question was soon indicated
publicly. The corporation was charged with creating a
subsidiary to be responsible for developing the
hydroelectric resources in the area. Hydro-Quebec, under the new law, must hold 51 percent of the shares in
this subsidiary and the corporation 40 percent, and three
of the five directors must be named by Hydro-Quebec.
This subsidiary also is ordered by the law to sell the electricity it generates only to Hydro-Quebec. This was the
main fruit of the battle waged in the legislature by the
Parti Québecois and was meant to assure a dominating
role in James Bay work for Hydro-Quebec. But when
Hydro-Quebec came to name its three directors to this
subsidiary, Bourassa would not accept them. He refused
to have Robert Boyd, an engineer, nominated for the
presidency of the subsidiary by Hydro-Quebec. Instead
he named Nadeau as president of the subsidiary, and
Charles Boulva, an employee of the James Bay Corporation, as a board member. Roland Giroux was
named to the subsidiary as well as to the corporation.
The other two members were not expected to give any
trouble to the government — especially Paul Dozois, the
man who was finance minister during the last melan-
choly corrupt years of the Duplessis dictatorship in
Quebec in the late fifties, and who had been awarded a
post as a Hydro-Quebec commissioner. This choice in-

dicated that Bourassa did not intend to entrust to Hydro-Quebec a leading role in development of James Bay, and renewed charges that behind the whole project was a desire to let private industry into the area to ripoff as much as it could of the natural resources of Quebec in the fine old tradition of the province.

Could Bourassa's refusal of Boyd have had anything to do with the latter's speech to the Electricity Club of Montreal in October? Six months after Bourassa had announced the project, Boyd began his speech unenthusiastically by saying: "You will be expecting some clarification from me (about the James Bay project). I regret to have to tell you that I am probably going to disappoint you. At the moment I cannot tell you how the work will be directed, what will be the number or the power of the generating stations to be constructed, what technique we will use to transport the energy, nor even what will be the timetable of work. We do not know so many things that you will be asking yourself what I can say to you on the subject of James Bay." That was letting the cat out of the bag; two months later Boyd was blocked from the presidency of the energy subsidiary by Bourassa. But Bourassa later lost his battle with Hydro-Quebec, and accepted Boyd as president of the subsidiary.

The corporation may also create subsidiaries for the exploitation of petroleum, forest and mining resources, in which the corporation would hold 51 percent of the shares, and the publicly owned provincial organizations — the Quebec Petroleum Operations Company (SOQUIP), the Quebec Mining Explorations Company (SOQUEM) and the Quebec Forest Salvage and Operations Company (REXFOR) — would hold 49 percent of the shares. But this is not mandatory on the corporation, and there is nothing to prevent it from dealing directly with companies that might wish to exploit the area's riches.

Under the act, almost nothing can move in the area without the authority of the James Bay Development Corporation. It has been given power to expropriate "any water-power, immovable or other real right" in the territory, even those not subject to expropriation under general law; to operate any means of communication by land, air, water or telecommunication; and to make any agreement considered expedient with the government of Canada, any other province or any federal or provincial agency. Any rights granted to anyone in the area under acts governing mines, hydraulic resources, forests, fish, game, agriculture, colonization or tourism shall be valid only if the corporation's advice has first been sought. As administrators of the municipality of James Bay, the directors of the corporation may declare any un-organized community of 500 people a locality and ap-point five members to the local council, which may un-dertake such functions as the directors decide to delegate to it.

The environment and the Indians are mentioned only briefly in the new law: "The Corporation must see to the protection of the natural environment and prevent pollution of the territory," under section five; and "this act shall in no way affect the rights of Indian com-munities living in the territory." But since the rights of Indian communities in the area are not known — and have never been respected in this part of the world — this provision is virtually meaningless.

The environmental provision has no real teeth, ac-cording to some lawyers who have studied the act. It is nullified by later sections providing that several acts un-der which environmental protection could be assured are specifically excluded from having authority over the corporation (for example, the Water Courses Act, which deals with trees that cannot be cut down and dams that cannot be built except under certain conditions). The same section says, "saving inconsistent provisions in the act, it shall not be interpreted as restricting the application of laws respecting mines, hydraulic resources, forests, fish, game, agriculture, colonization or tourism." This provision requires a judgment as to what provisions of the act would be regarded as "inconsistent" with its main purpose. And about that there seems little doubt. The act is designed to set up a body for developing hydroelectric power, and if anything is to be regarded as inconsistent with that purpose, it would most likely be the vague provision for respect for the environment.

People who tried to come to grips with the corporation during the following months found that the corporation, with its five directors, two coordinators and few secretaries, was rather an elusive body. Almost nothing, it appeared, was known about the James Bay area. The Canada Land Inventory, responsible for mapping the resources of the entire country, had stopped short of the southern boundary of the James Bay territory. The forest resources were only sketchily known; information about the mineral resources was locked away in the jealously guarded vaults of mining exploration companies; no inventory had been made of the animals. There was a great hole in the geological mapping of the area; soil maps did not exist. No one had bothered, during all seven years in which the project had been under consideration, to talk to the Indians, and now the corporation began to make slightly worried noises about how much good they hoped to do for the native people. So although the corporation talked airily about its mighty plans, it was quite impossible to measure this talk against any hard facts.

At an early stage the corporation commissioned a planning report with the object of "urbanizing and industrializing the region in an integral development led by the exploitation of natural resources" and, somewhat sadly bringing up the rear, "with respect for the conditions of the environment." It was a sort of child's guide to planning methodology, replete with maps showing James Bay in relation to Prudhoe Bay, Rio de Janeiro, Moscow, London, the Sahara desert and other "great world economic centers."

Twelve months after Bourassa made his announcement, studies were still underway to determine whether James Bay power would be economical. The implication was that if it were discovered to be too expensive, Bourassa would have to swallow his pride and cancel the whole show. But that presupposed that the consulting firms involved would have such saintly altruism as to report recommendations that would deprive them of the chance for millions of dollars' worth of work in the next decade.

Once the decision had been taken by Bourassa, all the later studies became to a greater or lesser degree exercises in self-fulfilling prophecy. There was never any doubt that the consultants involved could be trusted to come up with the right answers, as they had done a year before. When the decision in favor of the La Grande (or northern) project was announced in May, 1972, Bourassa was able to release twenty-five technical studies proving himself right. But the fact was that in the year after his political decision was made, $30,000,000 had to be spent on engineering studies designed to justify his decision. (None of them, of course, dealt with environmental or social effects of the project.) In May, also, the struggle between Hydro-Quebec and the James Bay Development Corporation became explicit before

the Quebec parliamentary committee. The corporation
and government wanted to hand over the management to
a consortium of private enterprise firms, excluding
Hydro-Quebec. But Roland Giroux laid down the facts
of life with unusual brutality: there would be no problem
financing the project, he said, on the express condition
that its management was confided to Hydro-Quebec. In
other words, only Hydro-Quebec could command the
confidence to attract foreign investment. And Hydro-
Quebec would not lend its aid unless it was to run the
project.

Was Hydro-Quebec, people began to ask, a state
within a state? Would management of the project by
Hydro-Quebec — an organization with a vested interest
in its own growth — assure that the project was in the
public interest? The La Grande project alone was now
estimated to cost $5.8 billion, a figure which supported
the growing suspicion that the cost of the entire project
had magically grown toward the $10-billion mark. The
government claimed that the northern decision was
made partly on social and environmental grounds: not
only would the engineering there be easier, but fewer Indians would be disturbed, and the environmental consequences would be less. Nevertheless, from the environmental point of view, even less is known about the
La Grande area than the NBR area. And the government's claims are not based on a single minute of
ecological study. The federal-provincial task force on environmental consequences said that so little was known
about the north that they could express no opinion on it.

So with the clarifications of May, 1972, the people of
Quebec were confronted with a denser fog than ever.

4. It's Their Land

The land that has been taken over by the James Bay Development Corporation is now and always has been occupied and used by the Cree Indians. They were there on the coast when Henry Hudson sailed into James Bay in 1611. They were there and wandering throughout the region when Father Charles Albanel, who seems to have been the first man to have gone overland to James Bay, made his trip by way of Mistassini at the headwaters of the Rupert in 1672. Before the white people arrived, these hunters and trappers moved across the land in family groups. They felt the impact of the white man before they were in contact with him — they were ravaged by his diseases. The diseases spread from Tadoussac and other trading centers as the white man's trade goods were handed from band to band far into the interior to places where the white man had never penetrated. The continuity in their way of life following their contact with whites is every bit as striking as the changes that occurred. They continued to live in family groups, though with a tendency to cluster around the trading posts at the river mouths on the bay; they continued to hunt and trap. Though they were Christianized by the Anglican missionaries, they continued to live a life of sacred contact with the animals with which they had reached so delicate a balance. They did not even take much of the white man's food until late in the nineteenth century, and then only staples such as flour, tea and lard.

The Cree were never conquered in that land, and they never sold it or ceded it by treaty or in any other way. They did not learn English, and they live today in 100-percent Cree-speaking communities, something that is rare even among the isolated Indians of northern Canada. (For example, the language of the Kutchin Indians in the ostensibly much more isolated Yukon Territory is much closer to disappearing than is Cree in northern Quebec.) These Indians remained totally alien in their first two centuries of contact with the white man. They were loosely organized, having no chief, suprafamilial authority or set body of rules and legal procedure for resolving conflicts.[1] Until this day they have remained nonassertive, inward rather than achievement-oriented, exercising deep internal controls over the expression of aggression, fear, pain and hunger.[2] They abhor boasting or any form of self-aggrandizement, exhibit quiet endurance in the face of hardship, are reticent in self-expression, and have a general hesitancy to intervene in the lives of others.

Until the late fifties they showed a remarkable adaptability in taking what they needed from the white man's civilization, and rejecting what they did not need. And they maintained the coherence of their culture to a really surprising degree. But since the early fifties they have come under pressures which they were, by the very reticence of their nature, ill-equipped to handle. Since then, every type of enterprise in the Canadian north has been given preference over the fur trade on which the native people depend. This has made trapping, even on a subsistence basis, difficult for them. The difficulty was compounded when their children started attending school and the parents had to stay in the reserves to look after them instead of going, as usual, into the bush.

The coherence of the Cree Indian value system has always been admirable, though it is only now coming to be properly appreciated as the incoherence of the white man's beliefs is being written in the degenerating quality of his urbanized life. But this coherence has been under pressure from the white man since communications — roads, railways, and airstrips — moved into the area in the wake of mining developments, which themselves followed the provision of government services to these remote Indians. The very loose organization of the Indian groups has always given the white trader a position of some authority in the villages that grew up around the trading posts. These people insulated the Indians from outside contact.[3] The Hudson's Bay Company was known to the Indians as *auchimau*. When company posts closed, as in 1965 at Waswanipi in the southern part of the James Bay project area, the Indians tended to drift away and attach themselves to other white intermediaries scattered along the road that runs across this northern country and connects Abitibi with the Lake St. Jean region. They were in search of a new *auchimau* — a fruitless search, as it now appears.[4]

The attitudes of the white society to these Indians have always been, to put it mildly, colonialist and superior, and in recent years brutally arrogant. For the Quebec government the Indians can scarcely be said to have existed. Quebec is unusual among Canadian provinces in that it has never really controlled and administered its

Beaver pelts drying at Rupert House after the trappers' return in February. This is th time of preparation for the spring goose hunt.

When the moose-hide is stretched on a frame, the women begin the back-breaking tas of scraping and preparing it for its eventual use in snowshoes, moccasins, etc.

own northern regions. These were originally part of the Hudson's Bay Company territory known as Rupert's Land, which was ceded by the company to the Crown in 1870. The southern limits of the company's territory were never clearly established, but the northern border of Quebec was extended by parallel acts of the Canadian and Quebec parliaments in 1898 as far as the Eastmain River — bang in the middle of the James Bay project area — and further extended to include the whole Ungava peninsula by the Quebec Boundaries Extension Act of 1912.

The Indians are now claiming that they have legal rights over all this northern land — and indeed over much of the province of Quebec — rights which have never been extinguished by agreement. These rights have been ignored by both the federal and Quebec governments, but the Indian case was given a boost in 1971 when the Dorian Commission, a commission of inquiry established to examine the territorial integrity of Quebec Province, found that the Indians have real and incontestable rights to much of Quebec, although these rights are limited to the right to hunt and fish for subsistence. This commission suggested that the Indian rights could be extinguished by the payment of the sum of $34 million to the Quebec Indians as compensation for what they have lost; the Indians of Quebec Association, which does not agree that Indian rights are so limited, has asked the government for $5 billion.

Historically, both in the United States and Canada, British colonial governments undertook to deal with Indian land rights in a fair and equitable way. And it was because of the government's recognition of these aboriginal rights that the treaties were made with Indians in Canada, the major ones beginning in 1871 within four years of the founding of Canadian confederation. These treaties covered most of the country, but not Quebec, British Columbia or the Maritimes. And the Indians now claim that the government is still under an obligation to deal with them about their rights in Quebec.

The Indian case rests on a series of documents and proclamations by various governments. The articles of capitulation of Montreal in 1760 provided that the Indian allies of the French king were to be maintained in the lands they inhabited if they chose to remain there. Following the Treaty of Paris, the Royal Proclamation of 1763 created an Indian territory reserved exclusively to the Indians as their hunting grounds. These rights were immune from provincial interference and extinguishable only by the Crown in right of Canada. When the Hudson's Bay Company lands were added to Canada in 1870, an Imperial Order-in-Council provided that "any claims of Indians to compensation for lands required for purposes of settlement shall be disposed of by the Canadian government . . . ." This was not mentioned when the territory was attached to Quebec in 1898. But when the northern sections were added to Quebec in 1912, the undertaking was specific. The province agreed to "recognize the rights of the Indian inhabitants . . . to the same extent, and will obtain surrender of such rights in the same manner, as the government of Canada has heretofore recognized such rights and has obtained surrender thereof," such surrender to be made or obtained only with the approval of the governor-in-council. The act also provided that "the trusteeship of the Indians in the said territory and the management of any lands now or hereafter reserved for their use shall remain in the government of Canada subject to the control of Parliament."

No treaty was ever made with the Indians by the

Quebec government in fulfillment of this obligation, though a similar undertaking of the Ontario government made in a similar act at the same time was fulfilled. Within two weeks of Bourassa's announcement of the James Bay project, a lawyer acting for the Indians of Quebec Association wrote to the deputy-minister for Indian Affairs, outlining the legal case and suggesting that both Canada and Quebec "are under an obligation to enter into agreements with the Indians in the project area in respect to their territorial rights.

"It would also seem," he wrote, "that there has been undue delay in the fulfillment of these obligations on the part of the Crown. It would seem primordial that the question of territorial rights of the Indians be settled immediately and before the project has developed much further . . . . It would seem that the Crown in right of Canada as the guardian of the Indian interest would be obliged to exercise all legal resources available to it, including court proceedings, to force the resolution of this problem and possibly suspend any attempted project work in the area pending settlement of the Indian claims. It is also likely that the Indians themselves might have a direct recourse at least by petition of right to force the resolution of their territorial rights, but this recourse would be directed against the Crown in right of Canada."

Unlike the United States, Canada does not have a large body of Indian case law; it was only in the last few years of the sixties that a number of lawyers began to investigate the real nature of aboriginal rights. Then, too, for the first time, Indian political associations funded by the federal government could afford to hire lawyers. The interest in aboriginal rights increased in 1969 when the Indians decided, after a long consultation process with the federal government, that they did not want to think about future policy until they had themselves researched the nature of their aboriginal rights in detail.

Having aboriginal rights in the use of the land has brought little benefit to the Indians of Canada because most of the treaties signed in the past (as the Manitoba Indian Brotherhood pointed out in a brief in 1968) were unconscionable transactions in which the white government negotiators took advantage of the Indian negotiators' failure to understand English, and inability to read or write. The Indian concepts, too, it is quite clear, were utterly different from those of the government men. Although they occupied the land, they had little sense of ownership. When the white men came, the Indians thought there was plenty of land for everyone. They moved over, welcomed the newcomers, and soon found themselves, at least metaphorically, looking down the barrel of a gun.

The persistence of the Indian right in northern Quebec has never stopped the Quebec government from encouraging people to move into that territory. The Indians had to struggle for a long time even to be granted enough land on which to build their houses. But if a mining operator discovered a mineral, he could get title to the land for a mine within a matter of days. The Quebec government has just never been interested in the native people of its northern territories. It was the federal government which first began to provide services to the Eskimos in arctic Quebec as part of its routine tours of the Northwest Territories. And until 1960, this was perfectly all right with the government of Quebec. In fact in 1939, the then Quebec premier, Maurice Duplessis, forced a case to the Supreme Court to try to prove that Eskimos were Indians within the meaning of the British North America Act, and therefore that those in northern Quebec were the responsibility of the federal government. He won his case, too.

Once again it was René Lévesque — the creator of Hydro-Quebec when he was minister of natural resources in the Lesage government — who changed all this. Levesque went into the north and told the Eskimos: "Let's face it, you've been treated like cattle. We're going to kick out the federal government, and you can become Quebecers like the rest of us" (or words to that effect). He no doubt meant well. But the native people in the north were deeply suspicious of the Quebec provincial authorities. They had been exposed only to the English-speaking establishments of the Hudson's Bay Company, the Anglican church and the federal government, and the French-speaking, Catholic Quebecers who had never done anything for them. Quebec and Canada made an agreement in 1964 under which the federal government would hand over its administration to the province. Levesque fell from power in 1966 before he had a chance to put the agreement into operation. Then Quebec began to build up an infrastructure of its own. By 1969, when the agreement was resuscitated, every little village in Nouveau Québec had two schools — one French-speaking provincial school and one English-speaking federal school. The Eskimos in that year said they did not want to change masters. With the advent to power of the strongly federalist and antiseparatist Trudeau, the federal emphasis changed. The federal government decided it might be well not to withdraw: its representatives said they would maintain their services (and indeed strengthen them) until such time as the Eskimos asked them to leave.

Much of the James Bay project area falls within the boundaries of Nouveau Québec. This background is an important element in what is happening today, for the native people — totally English speaking and completely unassimilated to the new, nationalistic Quebec — are being used as pawns in the struggle between the federal and provincial governments. Their interests are not the main concern in this argument. What is involved, rather, is a question of territorial jurisdiction, part of the endless tug-of-war that goes on between Ottawa and Quebec. It has even been suggested that Ottawa is strengthening its presence in Nouveau Québec as an insurance against the possibility that Quebec might one day opt for independence from the rest of Canada. In that case, suggests one author,[5] the federal government would be able to argue that Nouveau Québec was ceded to the province on condition that it deal with native land claims. Because that had never been done and because the province had never effectively occupied or administered the territory, the federal government would claim the province has no real legal claim to the territory. This sort of argument is very far from concern for the defence of the native people. But it is one of the most important elements in the touchy question of how the federal government is likely to react to the James Bay project.

On the one hand the federal government wants to keep up its guard in case of a deterioration in relations between Quebec and the rest of the country; on the other hand, the Trudeau government does not want to rock the boat for Bourassa, who may be the last possible reliable federalist premier in contemporary Quebec. So the federal government has "kept a low profile" about the James Bay project. It obviously does not like it much. A strange look comes into the face of anyone in Ottawa to whom the project is mentioned. One is quickly made to understand that when he talks James Bay, he is talking politics, and politics on the upper level.

Thus the Indian Affairs Department took no initiative to defend the interests of the Cree in the James Bay area. When George Manuel, the president of the National Indian Brotherhood, wrote to Indian Affairs Minister Jean Chrétien in September, 1971, to draw his attention to his responsibility for the Indians of James Bay, he was told that the department was trying to determine "the nature and quality of Indian rights" in Quebec and in James Bay; that the Indians of Quebec Association was negotiating with the Quebec government; that Bourassa was about to present a working document to the negotiating meetings; and that after that the federal government would become involved with the association and provincial negotiators. In December, 1971, Chrétien said on television that the Indians didn't want to sell their rights in Nouveau Québec; they wanted to have land. "And I take the part of the Indians. We must respect their wishes. If they don't want money, and they want land, we are going to give them land." When asked if he had a responsibility toward the Indians in the area, he replied: "I am responsible for Indian lands, I am the trustee for Indian lands, so I must protect their interests. I hope the government of Quebec is going to offer them something that will satisfy them. If not I am going to be obliged to object systematically in the name of the Indians . . . . The right of the Indians to occupy any one place in Nouveau Québec is difficult to determine, because the problem has never been resolved, but if the problem had been resolved in 1912, the development of James Bay would be made without any difficulty."

Eventually the Indians overcame the reluctance of the federal minister to get involved. Under considerable pressure, he finally agreed to speak for them with the Quebec government. And by June, 1972, a process of negotiation had begun, with the federal government ostensibly supporting the principle that the Quebec government was obliged to make a land settlement with the Indians. It was the first time in living memory that such a thing had happened.

But could the federal government be trusted really to "go for broke" on behalf of the Indians? It seemed highly unlikely. The Indians have always been defenceless in the face of the white man's advance into the southern part of the James Bay project area which began in the fifties with the discovery of minerals just south of Lake Mistassini, the building of a road and the creation of the town of Chibougamau. The invading whites, confident in their technological power, and unquestioning in their automatic assumption of the superiority of their own values, believed they were doing great things for the Indians — rescuing them from the rigors of their trapping life, "educating" them by taking their children away from home and offering them work on the peripheries of the white man's towns. The embargo placed on the trapping of beaver in the Mistassini region at the beginning of the fifties made it necessary for these people to either go on welfare or try to find work. The Indian Affairs Department encouraged twenty-one younger men to go south to work for the Canadian International Paper Company, and thus began the long and unhappy experience of work in the white man's world. By 1958 most of the Indians who had moved back and forth doing these woods jobs had returned to the reserve to try to reestablish themselves as hunters. In 1953 some twenty-four Mistassini men for the first time obtained work as line cutters and stakers for mining exploration companies. Though the Indians are unusually skilled at this work, they have never received higher pay for their extra skills: indeed, anthropologist Ignatius La Rusic[7] reported in 1968 that no Indians had ever been placed on the fulltime payroll and thus given working conditions equal to those of white workers. The Indians from Waswanipi had a similar experience. They soon found they were always given the "bad bush" (which reduced their earnings by 50 percent) and the attractions for them of wage work were largely illusory. If they could stay at home, receive welfare of $100 a month, and find time to supplement their food supply by hunting, they would be as well off as if they worked for $300 a month away from home. For when away from home they could not hunt and were forced to feed their families with "store food" which cost $60 a week for a family with four or five children. Twelve years after first entering wage employment — and having done so because the drop in the fur market made trapping uneconomic for them — the Indians were still being employed on the same casual basis, doing the same menial jobs, as when they began. Reports La Rusic:

> They were cast in the role of a cheap labor force, available and willing natives in the new colony of the north. They could make up the needed gangs of unskilled labor. Convenient, for they were there year-round, an almost captive labor force, which did not have to be provided with any of the most fundamental demands of white workers from the south: job security, advancement, equivalent pay, steady employment, or even the dignity of being accepted as an equivalent member of the human race. The Cree Indians became an important asset to those who were developing the mining and tourist industries in the region.

While this was happening to the fathers, the sons and

daughters were going to school. The traditional pattern of life for the northern Cree sees the whole family go into the bush in October for the trapping, and sometimes not emerge until the following June. They pass the summer at rest in the reserve, preparing for the new trapping season. On the coast, this pattern varies slightly with the wildfowl migrations. The winter's trapping ends by February or early March so that the hunters can prepare for the arrival of the geese, on their way north to the Arctic in the spring. They spend their summer fishing, hunt the geese again as they move south in the later autumn, and then go into the bush to the trap line for the winter.

The need for someone to stay at home to look after children going to the reserve school has made a drastic break in this familial pattern. A hunter who does not have his wife with him can hardly do the job. She is responsible for looking after his camp, preparing the skins, cooking the food and keeping the children in order. Her work is as important as that of the hunter himself. Therefore the hunter often decides it is not worth his while to stay around the reserve all winter; he goes off to the bush and takes the family with him, yanking the children out of school. In this way the children learn a certain set of values, built around the life of their hunting father, only to find these values coming under great pressure from the white influences to which they are exposed when they return to school. If the education is to continue past elementary school, the children have to go south to a hostel. The pattern has been one of children shuffled around the country like so many bags of potatoes. And whole generations of Indians have now spent most of their lives from the age of six away from home.

Children brought up on the trap line become extremely self-reliant at an early age. From four or five years of age, small boys hunt birds and have their own special hunting bags for the animals they kill. They learn how to set rabbit snares, and set traps near the camp for small game. They must take their share in the chores around camp, help their parents lay spruce bough floors and gather wood. They soon learn how to handle themselves in the bush, to recognize the tracks of animals and to gauge the strength of the ice they are crossing. By the time they go to school they have absorbed cultural habits of self-reliance, sharing and consideration for others which make their adjustment to the grab-bang-and-slap aggressive world of the white child all the more difficult.

Suddenly children whose models of excellence have been their highly skilled but illiterate fathers have a different set of models held before them: businessmen, office workers, suburban-dwellers and school teachers. When they return with the white man's manners, having lost their bush skills and attained some of the aggressiveness of their school chums, their parents are bewildered. In the jargon of the anthropologists, the children have been polarized toward a white identity model.[8] According to the McGill Cree project study, this identity conflict so bewildered teenagers that it caused clinically observable symptoms of mental and emotional disturbance among two-thirds of the 108 teenagers examined. This is the sort of brutal improvement being wrought among the Cree people of the James Bay area through increased contacts with the white man.

The James Bay project, then, is nothing new for the Cree. They are used to being disregarded by the white man, and this immense project which they hear will flood their hunting lands and drive away their animals is different only in scale from everything that has happened before. The white man has operated for fifteen years on the assumption that the traditional Indian bush life is not worth living, and has done everything possible to destroy it. In the process the Indians in many parts of Canada have been turned into pathetic, degenerated hangers-on to the edges of the white man's towns. Yet the Indian values have proved extremely tenacious. When the Waswanipi post of Hudson's Bay Company closed it was naturally assumed in the south that the now-scattered Indians would give up hunting and take to wage work. Within six years this assumption seemed to be on the way to being disproved. The Indians had, it is true, attached themselves to the new *auchimaus*, but these new *auchimaus* had not produced the necessary results. The Indians had been the last hired and first fired in one enterprise after another. They still got all the bad bush. And by the late sixties, it could be seen that even a band which had lost its physical coherence and was in a bad way, prey to drunkenness, debauchery and idleness, had begun to swing back to the traditional trapping life.

Roads brought into the beautiful lakes and forests of northern Quebec thousands of white hunters, people who wanted to get out into the immense nature, and who probably didn't realize they were taking animals and fish that were needed by the Indians. At first these hunters stayed fairly close to the roads. But the Indians found that they could not make a living off the country which had been hunted the autumn before by white men. McGill University anthropologist Harvey Feit, who has made a close study of the hunting methods of the Cree of the Waswanipi band, said that in the 1969-70 season one family tried to hunt a ground that had been exposed to white moose-hunters that year. "That is the only family that has ever reported to me that they were so short of food they had to come out of the bush back to town." By that time sports hunters were taking a third of the annual moose harvest. In still other respects the opening of communications to the area had a disastrous impact on the Indians. The logging companies now have huge concessions covering Waswanipi hunting grounds: of the 11,500 square miles of that band's grounds, one company's concessions cover 4,200 square miles. Since 1969 they have begun to clearcut very large areas, which is disastrous for the moose because they need a variety of different types of timber, including some tall stands for winter shelter. Cutting in patches would be compatible with subsistence use of the animal resources, and it might even improve the browse for the moose, which like young trees. But the present system takes no account of the needs of the animals or of the Indians. The Waswanipi hunting grounds will be heavily flooded: the reservoirs of Evans, Soscumica, Matagami, Waswanipi, Taibi and Olga will be situated in these hunting territories. As much as 1,000 square miles of their land will go under water, not to mention the spread effect, which will be described in the next chapter.

Feit's study shows conclusively that the Indians harvest the animal resources of the area by alternating hunting grounds, leaving some lying fallow for a year or perhaps two, and if necessary, switching from an animal whose population seems to be declining to one which is more plentiful. "What the James Bay project amounts to is a claim that the white people who go into the area will be the first to use the resources in a rational way," Feit told me. "But that is not so. The Indians have not been haphazard in their use of resources." Feit's figures show that despite the dispersal of the Waswanipi band, about half of the adult males had stuck to the hunting and trapping life. Of twenty-two hunting sections in the area, only six had been hunted the year before.[9] Most hunters either arrange to use someone else's territory, abandoning their own territory for a year, or divide their territory into sections, and use only parts of it in any one year. In every case the hunters who allowed their land to rest for a year took more beaver and moose than did those who hunted it the year before. Those who allowed the grounds to rest for two years took still more. The real proof that the Waswanipi carry out a planned and rational program of conservation is their hunting behavior in the territories that were hunted the year before: Feit's figures indicate that they hunted the animals at just below their level of productivity — that is, just below the level at which they were in a state of equilibrium. These conservation decisions are arrived at by the Indians through their remarkable closeness to the animals in their region. They are constantly evaluating the populations through the number of animals taken or seen, or the number of tracks seen. They take the least drop in these signs as an indication they are hunting too intensively, or have committed some other transgression for which the animals are holding them responsible. Feit found that all the Indians were convinced they could hunt more animals than they do. Their abstention has to do with a balance they strike between themselves and the animals on which they depend.

The introduction of white hunters upsets this balance and undermines the viability of the subsistence life that these people lead when on the trap line in the winter. The Indians take into the bush with them only staples — perhaps a few more than they took from the white man when they first came in contact with him, but the principles have not changed that much — and they catch the rest. When the hunting is good, they buy only 20 percent of their winter food. The rest comes from the bush. The most efficient animal is the moose, which provides them, according to Feit's figures, with 100,000 calories per man-day of work, compared with 16,000 to 20,000 calories from the beaver, 10,000 from fishing, and only 3,000 from small game. If the moose is not plentiful, they have to buy more food — up to 40 percent — and the percentage of their diet derived from small game and fish doubles.

It is astonishing, and terrible to report, that this delicately balanced subsistence life has been brutally hammered by decisions made callously by the Quebec government with complete indifference to the effect on the Indians. Through the sixties the Quebec government encouraged and licensed tourist outfitters to set up in the area, and finally the government built fishing camps of its own. Publicity campaigns were mounted to attract tourists. Now small towns such as Matagami, Chibougamau and Senneterre have planes ready to fly hunters deep into the bush to areas of high game population which have been spotted by pilots flying constantly in that region, an alarming addition to the pressure on the Indians' resources. Thus a deliberate decision was made to transfer the use of the animal resources from subsistence hunting by Indians to sports hunting by whites — from people who really need them to live on, to people who just want to kill them for fun. This was done without any consultation with the Waswanipi or Mistassini Indian bands. Worse than that, for several years in the late sixties the Quebec government carried out a policy of active harassment of the subsistence hunters — game wardens flew into the bush to the Indian hunting camps to seize meat taken by the Indians outside of the open season laid down by the white man's law. This open season takes place in September, before it is of any use to the Indian hunters, and is designed solely for sports hunters. Cruel though it may sound, when Indians in January or February killed a moose that they needed to live on, the government agents would fly into their camp, appropriate the meat and take it away. As far as is known, no prosecutions have been laid against white trappers for killing a moose for subsistence living.

"I did not know," Jimmy Mianscum, an Indian from Mistassini, wrote in 1969 when he appealed to the government to stop this practice, "why the game wardens came and landed at my hunting ground by aircraft while I was hunting in the bush. I did not know who send them to come at my camp.

"They ask for my meat. They took all my moose meat, and when I came out they were waiting for me where the plane landed, and of course again they took all my moose meat, what I had left. I told them I was a sick man, not in good health. This is the reason why I brought my food along with me, because I had to go in hospital and my family needed that food to eat. I was 40 miles out in the bush, that is where I brought the meat along from, to keep me going.

"They told me their boss or manager want that meat. And so I am short of food to eat. The food they took from me, it would keep me going at least one month. I did not understand any of this why they took my meat. They did not even tell me what's the reason they took my food."

It was not the first time Jimmy Mianscum had run up against the indifference of the white society. He was the hunter whose hunting ground stood where the mining town of Chibougamau now stands. The white men built a road. They built a mine, without asking permission. They put up a radar station on the hill on which he did his best winter hunting for moose. They poured sewage into the lake where he took his best fish. They never offered him a penny of compensation or explanation. He just had to move over, and get out, and he's been a casual laborer around the place ever since. This is racism — the sort of racism for which Canadians are so quick to condemn the United States. The supreme example probably was an incident reported by Judith Smith, a McGill anthropology student, in a study of Mistassini fishing camps. After the provincial government had produced a report on the decline of fish stocks in Lake Mistassini, the manager of a provincial government fishing camp decided, as his contribution to stopping the decline, that he would forbid the Indians employed at his camp to fish in the lake. Yet that season, these same Indians were employed in guiding white tourists to the lake's best fishing spots.

It is difficult for southern people to grasp this, but most of the enormous territory of the James Bay project — 110,000 square miles, at a fairly modest estimate — is covered by Indian hunting grounds. Their hunting method has an ecological foundation. Because in the northern latitudes the animal populations vary considerably, it is necessary for the human populations preying on the animals to vary, also. So they modify their numbers by spreading over a wider territory. The problem of maintaining this balance is compounded by the rapid increase in the human population. In 1915 in Mistassini, for instance, there were 175 people; in 1930, 228; in 1952, 450; and in 1971 there were 1,370. The 55,000 square miles of the Mistassini hunting area have been divided by the government into hard and fast areas given to each trapper for the purpose of hunting beaver, which is controlled. Most of the region is covered by beaver reserves, an action which became necessary when the beaver began to disappear during the early thirties. It is still not quite clear why this happened, or why the system of Indian respect for the animals broke down then. But apparently there was considerable pressure for overtrapping, since prices were good, and the arrival of better means of communication put more pressure on the animals than they could bear. The hunting territories as described by Indian hunters in 1971 to Toronto University anthropologist Adrian Tanner[10] are considerably different from those recorded several decades earlier. The Indian attitude toward the ownership of the land is still not properly understood by white investigators. The Indians speak of delimited trapping and hunting territories (for instance, they mark traps near the limits of their territories by making a sign on a tree) but Tanner believes the relationship with the land and the animals is much more complex than a simple feeling of proprietorship. In a study of one group of seven hunters over ten seasons, Tanner shows that none of them used their own hunting territory every year. Hunter A used B's territory three times, C's twice and twice hunted right outside the region. Hunter B used A's territory twice, C's twice and G's once. Hunter E used his own territory in only three seasons of the ten and Hunter G used B's territory more than he did his own. Though the hunters speak of delimited territories, in fact they circulate on adjacent territories, and outside their immediate region.

The hunting territories seem to be inherited, not merely by sons from their fathers, but sometimes by neighbors, or distant relations, or even by someone who has looked after an old man who needed help on the trap line. From the complexity of these relationships it appears that it would be more accurate to talk of hunting zones than of delimited territories. Tanner suggests that the most significant element in this web of relationships is the special rapport with the animals established by older hunters. These are the *shamans* of the Cree, men regarded as having special powers. And Tanner says that the relationship established between these men and the animals defines the hunting territory in such a way that it is the animals which control the movements of the hunters. In a sense, then, they believe it is the animals which possess the hunting territories. The old men establish these special relationships with the assistance of magic, and it is through the agency of such a *shaman* that a younger trapper establishes the relationship with the animals so that he might kill them. When such a man dies it is not a perfectly defined territory which is handed on to the younger man who is his closest hunting partner, but his relationship with the animals. Most often this younger man is the old man's son. "But," writes Tanner, "even the parental relations between him who inherits and the dead proprietor do not have much importance. The only thing that matters is that the man establishes his residence in a region which is not delimited in advance, but which is defined by the movements of the animals."

Fundamental to this complex of attitudes is the system of respect that all these Indians show toward animals. If a dead animal's bones are treated without respect, that animal is in the future likely to go away, and only men with the greatest power will be able to make it come back. Harvey Feit[11] says that the belief system of the Waswanipi Cree — and apparently it is much the same throughout the James Bay region — amounts to a coherent set of ecological principles. These religious beliefs are all built around the relationship with the animals.

In the Cree cultural universe, most things, but especially the animals, winds and several other natural phenomena, are "like" people in that they act with intelligence, manifest their will, behave individually, understand men and are understood by them. The north

wind — *chuetenshu* — and the animals themselves give
the Indian what he needs to live on. "All the forces which
we call natural are to them personal," Harvey Feit says.
"Everything is like it is alive. Water is like being alive.
Lightning is a person. Even the man's gun, traps,
snowshoes are like being alive. They say these things are
active, they have powers, they are able to do things. It's a
personal world, man has social relationships of respect
and dependency, all these personal forces give them what
they need to live, and in return they have obligations to
these personal forces."

In late January *chuetenshu* brings the snow which ac-
cumulates to such depth that the moose's belly drags and
it is hard for him to run so the hunters can catch him.
Chuetenshu blows the snow thin so that the moose
cluster on high ground and can be easily located. It is
part of the conception of these forces as persons that they
can be whimsical — thus when *chuetenshu* brings
weather that is too cold, the snow hardens and
snowshoes make so much noise that the moose is warned
of the hunter's approach. Later in the winter, warm
weather makes the snow slushy and difficult for the Indian to travel through. The intermittent return of
chuetenshu brings the cold that gives the snow an ice
crust through which the moose find it impossible to run.
In these many ways *chuetenshu* gives the animals to the
Indians. But because about half the moose die along the
shores of rivers and lakes and are discovered by the Indians when they are on their way to do other things, there
is a sense in which the animals give themselves to the Indian, too. Why, the moose gives himself to the Indian
even in the way he reacts to noises: he does not bolt away,
but stands, looks up, waits until he can see or smell
something, and in that moment of stillness and delay,
allows the careful Indian hunter to kill him.

The bodies of the animals nourish the Cree, but the soul returns to be reborn so that the men and the animals remain in equilibrium. Though the animals are killed they do not diminish, and both survive. The equilibrium is reciprocal and in return the men must act reasonably and with respect toward the animals and *chuetenshu*. What they must do is eat everything they have been given, and observe the rituals of capture, slaughter, consumption of the flesh and treatment of the bones. This means they have to kill the animals quickly so they do not suffer, they must never kill more than they need (though they are able to) and they must not play with the animals by killing for pleasure or self-aggrandizement.

Although the hunter gets only what is given to him, what is given to him is a function of what he has done to deserve it. Feit found that most hunters, when asked to explain their success or failure, still refer to the way they hunted the year before. If a hunter fails to capture an animal, he will usually say it is because either *chuetenshu* or the animals have decided they do not wish him to get what he wants, usually because of something he has done — one of his most important responsibilities being that he must not kill too many animals. If the animals are not being caught, it is because they have become angry and do not want to be caught; if they are left for a year or two they will cease to be angry, and will again consent to be caught. Though this is not a scientific view of the world, says Feit, "apparently the Waswanipi are preoccupied by ecological relationships. Evident ecological principles are part of their vision of the world."

Into this finely balanced ecosystem in which man has been and still is so intimately connected with nature, the white man blunders with total insensitivity, arrogance and indifference. While politicians in Canada spout about the need to build a multi-cultural society, and Canadians boast they have not built an American melting pot, but a Canadian mosaic, the reality is something else — the James Bay project is conceived and designed as if the Indians did not exist. Their needs are of no significance compared with the need of the southern white society for power. The Canadian society, apparently, is best served by smashing this remnant of a nature-oriented subsistence life, and turning all its practitioners into wage earners. A group of people who are demonstrating in their daily lives many principles which North Americans are gradually coming to realize they have abandoned at their peril, are to be swept aside almost as if the whole matter of public choice were dominated by some power whose wrath cannot abide the tenacious resistance of the Cree to the assumptions of the white, Christian(!), technological, acquisitive and dynamic society. Lip service, of course, must be paid to the value of the Cree perceptions, and to the awareness that the southern politicians, project directors and scientists have of the dangers facing the Cree. The James Bay Development Corporation from an early moment showed it was aware of the possibility of trouble from the Indians — or about the Indians — if it did not handle the matter carefully. It decided it needed "an information program" to give the Indians "objective information" about the project. The Indians of Quebec Association, beginning to feel its way in negotiations with the government, decided the best thing was to refuse to cooperate until it was surer of its ground. The corporation hired a man to get the "information program" under way. He found it difficult to get in touch with the Indians in the area, and when he did they found it difficult to understand what he was saying. Everything would be all right, he told them, if only they would trust him. He was for them. He would run interference for them inside the corporation. The Indians wondered, was he not working for the corporation, trying to sell the project to them? Whose side was he on?

The ecological task force (see following chapter) did not concern itself directly with Indians, though naturally the effect the project would have on the Indians swept in and out of the task force's ken as its members tried to pull together some of the likely effects in their two months of file reading. They came to the conclusion that the only potentially alarming environmental effect of the project would be the effect on the Indians, and recommended that something be done to try to minimize that effect. But the brief section devoted to Indians reeked of the typical colonialist white mentality which has degenerated Indian life all across the Canadian north:

Indians in the area are, economically and politically, strongly dependent on white man's society. Fishing, hunting and trapping are still important social and economic activities in the life of the region, but the Indians are no longer as economically dependent on them as some people think. Their economic dependence on the white man is characterized by this deficiency in traditional income and the availability of social welfare; their political dependence is expressed through the Indians of Quebec Association. Resource management projects in the James Bay area will undoubtedly accelerate the modification of the Indian way of life, either beneficially or detrimentally.

Not a suggestion that the Indians already have been managing the resources, and that the proposal is to take the resources they control away from them.

The invasion of the territory by an alien population
will upset native cultural patterns and traditions.
This could result in the disintegration of the
existing social structure and the alienation of communities or individuals.

And then they move on to the next page, where they ex-
patiate on the wondrous possibilities for tourism in the
area.

Professor R.F. Salisbury, director of the anthropology
of development program at McGill University, at an
early stage suggested to the James Bay Corporation that
it should make it possible for Indians themselves to
make their own independent investigation of the effects
of dam construction on their livelihood in the boreal
forest, since, as he wrote in a letter to Dr. Goldbloom,
the Quebec minister in charge of environmental protection, "the Indians have a close awareness of specific
relationships which biologists are only now finding to be
accurate." He told the task force:

We ought not to forget that the Indians have much
greater knowledge of the ecology of the region than
anyone else, and they also have the greatest interest
in knowing the changes that will occur. . . . The
knowledge of Indians of behavior of the beaver, of
the succession of vegetation in burned areas, for
example, is not expressed in terms employed by
scientists. But a program of ecological research
done by the Indians could have an extraordinary
importance both long and short term.

The oldest have seen important changes in the
forest, following the fires of 1900, the return of the
moose to the south around 1925, the near-
extinction of the beaver in 1940. They have ob-
served since 1955 the extraordinary effect of the
arrival of white communities, mines and forest in-

dustries. They also know what happened at Gouin reservoir.

He suggested that use be made of younger Indians who have a command of both English and Cree as agents through which the knowledge of the Indians could be communicated to outsiders needing that knowledge. "Without their participation face to face with ecologists, their influence will remain hypothetical."

Though the task force did pay passing heed to the probable destruction of the Indians, on the whole it seemed to be fairly convinced that the Indian life was already dead, and should perhaps be finished off. This opinion was not very well substantiated by scientific proof, although the task force members apparently leaned heavily on the report published in 1968 by the McGill Cree Developmental Change Program. (They may also have been influenced by the fact that most of the French-language studies of Indians in Quebec have been of communities whose traditional life has been severely disrupted by contact with whites, such as those on the north shore of the St. Lawrence.) The major question posed by the McGill research, done for the federal government's ARDA program (Agricultural and Rural Development Agency), had been how to maximize economic, social and political opportunities for the northern Cree "without destroying their right to be culturally different." Many of the underlying assumptions of the researchers who worked on that study are now felt to have been slightly colonialist themselves. They studied the Indians only from the point of view of their interaction with white structures, and devoted themselves to trying to suggest ways in which the Indians could adjust successfully. Norman A. Chance, who headed that project, had very much in mind the possibility of intervention by sympathetic whites, which

would stimulate the Indians to action. The major recommendations — for establishment of economically viable
reserves, an economic development corporation, a
revamped education structure — all view the possible
solutions as being generated from outside the Indian
communities.[12] Now, as research into Indian perceptions
has become more sensitive and profound, the
inadequacy of this approach is beginning to be understood. The idea that it might be the white people who
would have to adjust to the Indians was given little attention in the McGill project, because it was considered
unrealistic. Nevertheless, in the early months of the
argument about James Bay, that idea seems to be taking
hold. We are beginning to see the development of an Indian leadership which is ready to pressure its own
association and outside white structures as well.

It may be too little, and too late, and after all, a hand-
ful of Indians whose only concern is the northern environment of which they are an integral part can hardly
be expected to compete in the corridors of power with $6
billion or $10 billion of Wall Street money. The
significant development, however, is that the Indian
response now is based on Indian perceptions of what life
is all about, and it is the white men who are being slowly
educated about the effects of their own headlong and
precipitate behavior.

The real balance of government and James Bay Corporation interest is demonstrated by $60,000,000-worth
of construction contracts having already been awarded
by the end of 1971, while a contract for $26,365 had
been given to Dr. Salisbury's group to produce a report
(again within two or three months) on the effects the
project would have on the Indians in the area. Even this
small program was delayed because of an argument
between Dr. Salisbury and the corporation about

the researchers' right to publish the results. Dr. Salisbury, who would undertake the study only with the agreement of the Indians, would report his projections about the impact of the project directly to the Indians. The corporation's objection to this was neatly summarized by one of its executives: "That would be social animation, and we do not want any social animation. We want the Indians to get objective information." The corporation finally accepted Dr. Salisbury's necessity for contact with the Indians, and Salisbury agreed any recommendations he might make would be kept secret for three years. The extraordinary lengths the corporation directors went to to achieve this secrecy is surely a revealing indication of their sincerity toward the Indians.

Finally, in January, 1972, corporation members did manage to get together in a meeting with representatives of the northern communities. They agreed their information team would not go into the area before the two communications workers hired by the Indians of Quebec Association, and that when they did go, the two teams would travel together. One Indian Association worker was young Phillip Awashish, senior counsellor of the Mistassini band. He had attended McGill University, gone through the white man's educational system with ideas of becoming an engineer and had finally, as he says, got his head back together by returning to live on the reserve. The other was Chief Billy Diamond of Rupert House, a twenty-two-year-old who had taken over the leadership of his band from his father. These two men spent some five weeks in the south trying to discover what was involved in the James Bay project. But the corporation's team could not wait for this research to be completed. They took the Cree-language version of the ecological task force report, and went north to distribute it. When in February the two communications workers began their trip through the communities, they learned the people had not been able to understand the Cree syllabics in which the translation was made. There are two dialects of Cree: Eastern Cree, which is spoken throughout the Quebec area, and Moose Cree, spoken west of James Bay. In Mistassini the Indians decided the syllabics must have been written in Moose Cree. But at Rupert House they met some people who knew Moose Cree, and they couldn't understand the translation either.

At a meeting in Rupert House on February 21, 1972, the gentle, retiring and unassertive Cree people finally took an action which quickly began to reverberate through their communities, and through the minds of all the young Indians from northern Canada. The chief's sister, Annie, who had just returned from the trap line the day before, tried to read aloud the Cree version of the ecological report. It was only a smidgen of the whole report, a mere 15 pages, compared with the 55 pages of the English-language version, not to mention the nearly 300 pages of the first draft. And the Cree version did not include the somewhat insulting paragraph (quoted above) so haughtily describing the Cree dependency on the white man. It was obvious that plenty had been left out.

What Annie Diamond read out to the meeting was totally incomprehensible to the Cree-speaking people there. The dots between the vowels had been omitted, so the words didn't make any sense. "We can't understand this thing," cried the chief. "What will we do with it?"

"It should go in the fire," yelled a man in the audience. Suddenly the air was thick with flying copies of the Cree-language version of the federal-provincial task force report on the environmental consequences of the

James Bay project. There was an air of liberation, almost of carnival, as the Cree gathered up the books and stuffed them into the wood stove. Then they gathered up more armfuls, took them outside into the snow and made a big bonfire of them — Canada's first book burning in many years. It was a curiously satisfying event. The Cree who lived with and understood nature in all its complexity, who loved it and wanted to preserve it, were declaring roundly that they were not fooled by the meretricious propaganda prepared by civil servants, dressed up as science and served to the Indians by the James Bay Corporation, with such an air of sanctimonious righteousness that even the continent's most reserved and gentle people couldn't stomach it any more. In that one act they put the whole argument about the James Bay project into perspective. In the weeks that followed, one by one, the Indian communities rejected the report; they were not going to allow the southerners to pull the wool over their eyes this time. A month later, Crees from the Waswanipi band began to post their copies back to the James Bay Corporation, accompanied by polite little notes in Cree, explaining they were sorry, but they were unable to understand the report.

Notes For Chapter IV:
1. Jean Trudeau, "The Cree Indians," p. 135, *Science, History and Hudson Bay*, published by the Department of Energy, Mines and Resources, Ottawa.
2. N.A. Chance, p. 19, *Developmental Change Among the Cree Indians of Quebec*, printed by Department of Regional Economic Expansion, Ottawa.
3. Same as 2, p. 12.
4. *The New Auchimau, A Study of Patron-Client Relations Among the Waswanipi Cree*, a research report by Ignatius La Rusic for the Cree Developmental Change Project, April, 1968.
5. Leonce Naud, article in *Le Devoir*, February 11, 1972.
6. Quoted by Naud in *Le Devoir*.

7. *Hunter to Proletarian*, research paper by La Rusic for Cree Developmental Change Project.

8. See a series of papers by Peter S. Sindell and Ronald M. Wintrob for the Cree Developmental Change Project.

9. See article, "L'ethno-ecologie des Cris Waswanipi," in the special issue of *Recherches Amerindiennes au Quebec*, devoted to *La Baie James des Amerindiennes*, December, 1971.

10. See article by Adrian Tanner, "Existe-t-il des Territoires de Chasse?" in *La Baie James des Amerindiennes*, December, 1971.

11. Same as 9.

12. *ARDA* report on Developmental Change Among the Cree Indians of Quebec.

5. Progress, Progress

Canada has 45 of the world's 305 man-made lakes measuring more than 100 square kilometres each, but nothing is known about their biology. No studies have been made of the behavior of the water, or the effect of water impoundment on temperature, quality or turbidity; of the effect of impoundments and water fluctuations on the food chain from the plankton on up to the fish; of the climatic effects on the surrounding countryside, or the effect of sedimentation on the watershed and on shorelines adjacent to the river mouths. Though for many years Canada had the world's biggest man-made lake, the Gouin Reservoir, nothing is known even about it. This lack of information and concern about man's effects on biological systems is no doubt part of the intellectual and social climate which made it possible for a weak and irresponsible politician to rush so precipitately into the fantastic James Bay scheme. When Quebecers woke up one day to find that their north was about to be turned upside down in the biggest industrial project of its kind ever launched in North America, no one was equipped with the information on which to base an informed criticism of the scheme.

Naturally, in the current climate, so different even from the early sixties when Hydro-Quebec's great schemes aroused such pride in the Quebec breast, there was no lack of people ready to cry "Rape!" the moment the scheme was announced. And because governments always like to appear to be taking account of public opinion, the Quebec government began to protest its environmental virginity within a few days of Bourassa's announcement. Dr. Victor Goldbloom, the Quebec minister responsible for the service for environmental protection (a new government service), said that protection of the environment was one of the factors that had caused Hydro-Quebec and the government to choose the James Bay project rather than build thermal or nuclear plants in the cities. He had asked Hydro-Quebec, he said, for the studies they had undoubtedly made on environmental consequences during the several years of research they had done in the area.

It was not the last time that Dr. Goldbloom would be discovered speaking, as the Indians say, with forked tongue. He must have known that Hydro-Quebec had done no studies of any kind on the environmental impact, and that any future studies, if they were to be done, would necessarily follow the decision to go ahead, rather than precede it. A year later there was still no evidence to suggest that any information about environmental consequences had ever been gathered about James Bay before the Bourassa decision. Indeed, a year later a Hydro-Quebec study admitted there was no biological knowledge extant of the James Bay area. Yet, within three days of Bourassa's announcement, Goldbloom had said publicly he was trying to get the Cabinet to agree to establish a research team to formulate recommendations for the protection of the environment. A distinct credibility gap, then, had already opened up. On the one hand Goldbloom claimed that environmental considerations had been a factor in the decision; on the other he said environmental research was necessary.

This sort of inconsistency has dogged the issue from the beginning. People who have tried to come to grips with it have simply failed to get the necessary information. Citizens who worried about what they heard of the scheme from time to time gathered together in Montreal, Toronto and Ottawa. But they couldn't find out what was involved. In January people drawn together by seven conservation, wildlife and antipollution groups held a day-long workshop at McGill University at the end of which they declared all work on the project should be stopped, and no further money spent until the Quebec government had explained what it was up to. They said the social, economic and environmental implications were totally unknown and unexamined, and the Indians should be allowed to decide what they wanted to do with the region, and be given the time and facilities to enable them to make that decision.

No one took any notice of the McGill workshop. The machine had been put in motion by Bourassa on April 29, 1971; the full resources of the state and of industry were devoted to getting it clanking northward. Everything official being done was in the nature of justification for the scheme except for the lip service that had to be paid to environmental, social and economic virtues. Though everybody who has studied the man-made lakes schemes which proliferated throughout the world in the sixties agrees that years of basic research are necessary before any precipitate decisions are taken, Bourassa paid no attention. Though in the United States

biologists are normally given a lead time of five years
over engineers, Bourassa paid no attention. The decision
had been made, and now it must be justified on every
level — economic, social and environmental. Whatever
the dangers, it must be shown, by hook or by crook, to be
the greatest thing that could ever happen to the northern
Quebec ecosystem.

To this end the federal and provincial governments set
up a task force to examine the environmental consequences of the James Bay project. Evidently it grew out
of a meeting of about twenty people, mostly civil servants, held in Ottawa three months after Bourassa's announcement, to consider the possible effects of the
project. Only one of these twenty people had been in the
James Bay area. A participant later declared he could
have sat in his office and written out in advance a summary of everything that was said. Fisheries, soils and
forestry experts muttered away about how, if you flood
the land, the trees will die, how the beaver will disappear
if you destroy their habitat, how there will be a change in
sedimentation if you build a dam, and so on. From this
rather absurd meeting an exchange of letters arose between the federal environment minister, Jack Davis, and
the Quebec minister of natural resources, Gilles Massé.
They agreed to set up a task force composed mostly of
civil servants from the two governments to make a broad
evaluation of the project's impact on the region's environment, "taking into account that the depth of the
study will be governed by the time limitations involved."
The evaluation would identify the various elements in the
ecosystem to be affected; delineate their inter-
relationships and indicate their individual sensitivities
and their relative importance; formulate recommendations as to any preference from an environmental
impact point of view between the La Grande and NBR

schemes; recommend the nature and scope of a more intensive long-range study to be conducted in subsequent years; outline a methodology that could be followed; and suggest appropriate federal-provincial organizational arrangements.

The task force began work in September, 1971, and was asked to report by December. As the task force later admitted in its report, its membership was "somewhat indefinite, its activities characterized by informality, and its organization unsophisticated." It was, in essence, a bunch of federal and provincial civil servants charged with gathering from the files as much knowledge as they could scrape together, applying their experience to that knowledge and trying to make recommendations along the line given in their mandate — all within two months. To do them justice, most members of the task force seem to have realized that what had been undertaken was a scheme to modify nature on a really colossal scale, and that whatever they had to say about it would be equivalent to shutting the door after the horse had bolted. Dutifully, they gathered as much information as they could find and tried to bind it into a report. Because this information had very little scientific respectability, in that it was not based on actual research in the geographic area, the report was tentative and somewhat critical in nature, and its first, long version was set in a context which raised the question of the philosophy of development itself.

This question had been raised earlier in a paper written by André Marsan, an ecologist from the Montreal Centre of Ecological Research and not a civil servant, who had been appointed by Goldbloom as the Quebec coordinator of the task force's work. Marsan's paper began by recalling that in 1952 the International Union for the Conservation of Nature and Natural Resources

had declared that when any new projects, particularly
hydroelectric works, were under consideration, careful
studies should be made of all resources in the area
"before any plans for the construction or execution of
such an enterprise shall be decided. In twenty years we
have advanced very little, apart from the declaration of
principle, in taking real account of the ecological impact
of such works, and the committee is forced to repeat that
appeal in practically the same terms as in 1952," wrote
Marsan. He outlined in some detail the disastrous experience at the Aswan Dam and wrote: "Most of these
disasters were foreseen by specialists in anthropology,
sociology, pedology, epidemiology and public health as
well as by ecologists. But none of them had the power nor
the influence to make themselves felt at the decision-
making and political levels."

"Does man so overestimate his real power that he
wishes to cut the umbilical cord that ties him
irremediably to nature?" asked Marsan, a question
pregnant with meaning in the James Bay context. Then
he came to his main point: energy demand cannot continue to double every eight years, for soon we will arrive
at absurd and astronomical figures: "The committee
considers that advertising designed to accelerate consumption is a short-term policy and respectfully
proposes that this advertising should be reoriented to
promote sane consumption, without waste." Society in
general must understand that energy is a rare thing, according to present standards, and the committee
questioned whether economic profitability was a useful
standard in decisions about the management and conservation of resources, if the aim was to improve the
quality of life and the environment. Marsan admitted
there were difficult questions to answer, but at least the
present state of knowledge suggested we should be

ringing the alarm bells. "It is not just a question of the hydroelectric development of James Bay, but in the immediate future they are thinking of the Nelson and Albany Rivers, the Lachine Rapids (near Montreal) and Churchill Falls (in Labrador). The integration of all these effects could set under way a spiral of unprecedented consequences, on a scale presently unforeseeable."

He warned that the committee's recommendations for a system of ecological studies should be accepted by the planners and not considered as simple moral support designed to appease an increasingly strong and persistant conservationist opposition. It was certain that if the project did proceed, negative ecological impacts would be felt. "One cannot modify an ecosystem in so brutal a fashion," Marsan said, "without causing a process of degeneration or without obliterating numerous things. Society would have to pay for these negative effects, whether the loss is a directly economic one, or indirect, such as a loss of aesthetic character, natural beauty and so on." He ended with this warning: it was imperative that ecological studies should accompany the conception of the project, and the elaboration of the engineering project in all its phases. If not, ecologists would be reduced to the extremely secondary role of simply foreseeing consequences and proposing ways to minimize them.

Marsan's paper was published later in the working papers of the task force, which were placed in libraries and universities. It also formed an important contribution to the first draft of the task force report, but the more challenging parts of it bit the dust, and, like many other critical contributions, it was eliminated from the final report. The members of the task force, being loyal civil servants, were unable to raise the question of whether the James Bay project was desirable, and could not question the development ethic of society as a whole which Marsan had raised. It was supposed to be a task force of experts from environmental departments only, yet André Langlois, an engineer employed by the James Bay Development Corporation, sat in on several of the meetings, and appears to have played a major role in deciding what was and was not acceptable. The first draft of the report had included many preliminary papers forwarded to the committee outlining the concerns of various specialists, but most of these papers were eliminated from the final report. This clearly disturbed some members of the committee, for they took the unusual step of dissociating themselves from the fundamental questions as to the project's viability or desirability.

[The report] is an attempt to express the consensus of the knowledge and opinions of numerous people. It may contain views and value judgments to which not all members unreservedly subscribe. Furthermore, any statements expressed herein do not necessarily reflect the views of their respective government departments.

The task force has interpreted its mandate to be the making of a preliminary appraisal of the impacts upon the environment that can be anticipated due to the development of the James Bay project. It has not been interpreted as answering the question "From the environmental impact point of view, should this project proceed?" It is understood that the decision to proceed has been taken. This report therefore does not reflect any personal or collective reservations held by the task force members as to whether society really needs the project, whether there are more economical and less environmentally disturbing ways of harnessing energy resources to meet Quebec's future electric power requirements, or whether society should strive to restrain its electrical demands rather than increase its supply. It was assumed that these fundamental questions had been adequately considered by the authorities prior to making their decision to proceed.

This does not indicate that the members of the task force had much conviction in the quality of their own work. And no wonder, for the report they produced is a curious document, whose logic is almost incomprehensible. Its major recommendation is to turn James Bay into a vast ecological laboratory, swarming with researchers — mostly, no doubt, from their various government departments, or from the Centre for Ecological Research. Given that Canada has shown no interest at all in man-made lakes, despite plenty of opportunity to do so, this sudden enthusiasm is rather suspicious. The major impact, the report says, the only one of "potentially alarming proportions," would be on the Indian people of the area, and something should be done about it. Marsan's list of the detrimental effects of the Aswan Dam appears watered down to a recognition of some beneficial effects. And a conclusion is reached which appeared nowhere in the report's first draft: "In many respects a changed ecosystem may be just as satisfactory as the original natural system, and even produce side benefits to man. It is concluded that this will hold true for James Bay."

It is perfectly obvious that a good deal of arm twisting went into this conclusion. Additionally, it was used as the lead paragraph of the press release that accompanied the report's publication. Yet, despite this favorable conclusion, the task force lists page after page of studies which should urgently be done and information urgently needed, and it establishes quite clearly the appalling lack of knowledge with which the original decision to proceed was made. Though the report was presented to the public by Dr. Goldbloom as a scientific, not a civil service, work it can be seen that the members came to the only conclusions that were consistent with their status as government servants. Despite their lack of knowledge in so many fields, they nevertheless found it possible to conclude that the man-made ecosystem would be just as good as the natural one. Any other conclusion, of course, would have been deeply embarrassing to the Quebec government. Yet on the other major question put to them — whether the northern or southern part of the project was preferable from the environmental point of view — they pleaded that their lack of information prevented them from coming to a decision. After all, a political struggle was going on between the government and Hydro-Quebec about which scheme to start with, so any decision the ecologists made would have been an em-.barrassment. And civil servants are not supposed to embarrass their masters.

The masters are embarrassing enough, as it is. Goldbloom, Massé and Nadeau brought doublethink to a fairly high level at the press conference when they released the task force report. The government, said the ministers, accepted the task force report in its entirety and would implement it. Because the report says that data about existing environmental conditions should be collected before construction starts, would they now stop all construction in the area? Certainly not, replied Nadeau, the schedule would go on as planned. Because the report says that environmental studies should be integrated into engineering planning and construction, and no environmental studies have been made, was that not sufficient reason to halt construction? Certainly not, said Nadeau.

The government, then, accepted a report which implied construction should be slowed down; but it also accepted the continuation of construction. Talking with forked tongue is what the Indians call it.

This appalling lack of sincerity — this blatant attempt to use the cloak of the ecological task force as a shelter under which to justify the project — was even more starkly revealed in May, 1972. The only firm recommendation of the task force had been that the headwaters of the Caniapiscau should not be diverted, and the government said, yes, it accepted the report in its entirety. But in May the government decided to go ahead with the La Grande, or northern project, including the scheme to block the headwaters of the Caniapiscau.

The government is able to get away with it because most of the media in Montreal have shown no more inclination to subject the James Bay project to critical examination than has the Trudeau government. The whole Quebec establishment depends on Bourassa, and is hopping around uneasily from foot to foot, hoping that the premier hasn't blundered this time. If he has, they don't want to make it too obvious. "I find it rather sinister, and strange and suspicious that it is so difficult to get information on a project on which the government is going to spend $6 billion or $10 billion of public money," said Kari Levitt, an economist, at a public meeting held in March, 1972, to discuss the project and bring it to public attention. The hall was crowded with frustrated people who desperately wanted to know what was going on. But the meeting received very little publicity the next day; several major newspapers did not even mention that it was held.

The intellectual honesty of the task force report is very

much in question. A comparison of the first draft and the final report shows how the environmental effects have been fudged and obscured by being rewritten into vague civil service language. When all the smooth justifications have been taken into account, it remains true that mankind is about to make a major intervention, by any standards in the world, in the ecosystem of one-quarter of the province of Quebec — one which will involve many unknown effects.

Quite certainly the beaver and the moose, the main animals on which the Indians depend, will be either grossly reduced or even wiped out. Rupert Bay, at the foot of James Bay, and one of the three greatest resting and feeding places for geese in North America, will be drastically changed by the diversion of two of the rivers flowing into it. Yet nobody has given any consideration to the effect of the change on the birds. The impact of these huge diversions and impoundments of water and the flooding of thousands of square miles of habitat used by mammals and birds living at the area's extreme northern limits is completely unknown. Changes caused by sedimentation, erosion, variations in ground-water level, drying up of swamps, and flooding of new swamps can only be guessed at. Whether the interruption of the food chain — from terrestrial and aquatic plants and invertebrates to the fish, birds, whales, seals and polar bears of James Bay — will reduce animal life in the area is a matter for speculation. The only answer to these uncertainties that the progress-oriented people of the south can supply is: so what? In 1972, given man's increasing understanding of the fragility of his dependence on the earth's life-support system, this is not good enough.

"I have no hesitation in saying," declared K.A. Kershaw, of McMaster University in Hamilton, Ont., a plant biologist with an international reputation who recently has been carrying out studies on the Ontario side of James Bay, "that we do not have any biological knowledge of this area worth a damn, and I would be prepared to go into court and swear it under oath." Two recent publications written by Kershaw about growth patterns and water relations in lichen-dominated woodland in northern Ontario indicate that the relationships are so complex it is impossible to make a predictive model of the effect of any intervention in the system. The main scientific criticism of the ecological task force report is that it deliberately oversimplifies what are likely to be extremely complex effects, and comes out suggesting — loyal civil servants — that whatever the effects are, they will be manageable. The implication is, don't worry, everything's going to be all right.

The ecological task force report was based on the assumption that the NBR project would go ahead first. The report admitted frankly that almost nothing was known about the environment around the La Grande River, which is the center of the northern scheme that *is* now proceeding. But all of the effects mentioned in this chapter will be the same in the north as in the south, except that the soils are less unstable in some parts of the northern project area. Four huge dams are to be built along the La Grande River, the first of them about 72 miles from the coast at what is called LG 2. This lake will flood land for as far as 70 miles upstream from the dam; the flooding behind LG 3, which will be built about 150 miles from the coast, will extend nearly 140 miles upstream. The lakes to be created are vast. (For more detail about what is happening, see the last chapter.)

Above the dams the main changes will be in the flooding of a huge area of land, in the ground-water level, and in increased evaporation from the reservoirs. They will affect most life within the vicinity of the bodies of water. The Indians, the only people who really understand the behavior of the larger animals, have no doubt that the flooding of the land will destroy the animals. The ecological task force admitted that the habitat of the moose and caribou (the latter, migratory animals, are not numerous, but seem to have been making a comeback toward Fort George in recent years) will be affected. It has been estimated that 40 percent of the Indians will lose 50 percent of their hunting territories. But this grossly underestimates the effect of the flooding because any loss of moose population will have a disastrous effect on the Indians. The pressure on the moose will come not only from a decline in their summer browse around the edges of lakes and streams (possibly forcing them to use instead the upland browse of birch and willow which they usually reserve for winter), but also from sports hunters who will enter the area in greater numbers. The Indians depend on the moose for food during the winter; the increase in the Indian population has already put some pressure on the balance between man and moose. If the animals are reduced by any significant amount, it will finally end, once and for all, the Indian hunting life. Knowing this, it is difficult to understand how the ecological task force could say with such confidence that the Indians can "choose to maintain their traditional way of life" (page three of the English version). It is simply ridiculous for Pierre Nadeau, president of the James Bay Corporation, to say, as he did in a speech to the Montreal Chamber of Commerce on January 18, 1972, "From the economic point of view, it is undeniable that the indigenous people will profit first and most directly from the infrastructure that will be created." That is colonialist arrogance, and nothing else.

The Indians depend, too, on the beaver. This area

produces the world's highest quality beaver fur, and 20 percent of the Quebec crop. The effect on the beaver will be severe, depending on the area flooded and the size of the annual draw-downs. Beaver disappeared from Gouin Reservoir when it was flooded in 1911, and had not reappeared by 1944. (They were reestablished in 1952.) But again the federal-provincial task force minimized this impact. Without mentioning the experience at Gouin, it decided that the beaver "would not be greatly disturbed," and that any initial loss could later be compensated. (After, or before, the Indians have been moved away?) Perhaps the task force arrived at its conclusion under the influence of the James Bay Corporation official who suggested that the beaver could be moved away by helicopter and reestablished in unflooded areas — an idea the Indians regard as ridiculous. Most of the country is already carrying an optimal beaver population, so any transplanted beaver would be in competition for habitat with those already there.

Another effect of the dams that has been greatly minimized by official sources will be the likely changes in ground-water levels. The task force report says calmly, "A modification of the vegetation will occur where the water table rise is felt, and landscape pollution will occur in these areas as the trees die." This will very much increase the area of land affected by the flooding. No one knows how much. It could multiply the 4,000 square miles to be flooded by a factor of one or two. Russian experience[1] in country which is not unlike James Bay suggests that the effects of ground-water level changes can make themselves felt within a radius from twelve to thirty miles from the lakes. Artificial lakes in Russia have been found to change the level of ground waters as well as their flow velocity, chemical composition and, in certain cases, the direction of flow. When ground-water level rises — in James Bay it is already much higher than in the Russian reports — what happens is "gleying," swamping and salting of the soil (it becomes sticky, saturated and unproductive) while the trees (and animal populations) are affected. This means, really, that roots are just drowned. The spread of these effects depends on the permeability of the soil, and cannot really be predicted in James Bay. But if it is anything like twelve miles around the huge reservoirs that are being created, then we are taking the risk of creating a veritable wasteland. This may be an exaggeration; it may never happen. The real point is that the project is going ahead, before anyone really knows *what* will happen.

Certain people who have examined as much detail as the government has made public believe that when the water is reduced to the minimum by draw-down, vast areas of unsightly mud flats will be exposed to the eye. "At the new future maximum levels, most of the reservoirs will offer a desolate spectacle," said the draft report. "Thousands of heads of trees, dry, will be out of the water. And some of the reservoirs with variable levels will present a disastrous spectacle for a certain period of the year, mainly in spring before the runoff." These statements were eliminated from the final report, for they would certainly have made a bad headline, and enabled everyone to know that what is proposed in James Bay is about the same as what has been done with disastrous results in Lake Williston, behind the Bennett dam in British Columbia. If the lakes are to be drawn down fifteen or thirty feet, it does not take a vivid imagination to picture the result. The effect of these changes on predatory birds and animals — owls, hawks, martens, stoats, weasels — will be tremendous, though the effect on the seed-eating forest birds is not likely to be so great.

When the water levels rise behind the dams, fish will have to search for new spawning beds. All fish spawn in shallow water, anything from a few inches to a few feet deep. Most fish in the James Bay rivers are bottom-spawners, that is, their eggs drop to the bottom after being laid. They need to find sand bars or gravel beds because this sort of terrain holds the eggs and allows the water to circulate around them. Only two types of fish in the area lay eggs that float. The effect of the flooding of the swamps and muskeg will be to decompose the organic material on the bottom so that when newly laid eggs drop into this decomposing matter they will die. There will, therefore, be almost no year-class of fish in the early years after impoundment, despite an immediate increase in productivity of the lake. That usually means an increase in the growth of algae. The fish are adapted to the great flood of water in the spring and the decline in the summer; they are unlikely to adapt easily to the changed regime that the hydroelectric project will impose on the lakes. Even if they do succeed in laying eggs, a sudden draw-down of water will leave those eggs exposed on the lake's littoral. It is simply impossible to cover these effects by talking airily about minimum annual draw-downs. In practice, draw-downs of water for hydroelectric production follow a zigzag course: they are up one day, down the next, up again and down, and very few fish could survive this sort of treatment.

If the Russian experience is any guide (the Russians have studied the physicochemical changes in impounded waters much more than Canadians have) the decomposition of organic materials and the leeching of mineral salts from the flooded soils will in the first stage cause a severe reduction in the diversity of species among phytoplankton, zooplankton, benthic (bottom-dwelling) fauna and fish. In one Russian reservoir, only 56 of 150 benthic species survived nine months after flooding. Some fish species, usually the salmonids, are severely reduced in numbers, while coarse fish are heavily increased. Thus the balance of life in the lake is drastically changed, and despite many attempts made in Russia to reverse this process, or hasten the return to stability, they have never been very successful. Once the impoundment is made, the results that follow are almost inevitable. Man has not yet found a way to prevent them. The salmonids (whitefish, cisco, lake trout, brook trout) which spawn in the fall can all be expected to suffer but the northern pike, burbot and perch, which spawn in winter or early spring, might be expected to resist changes successfully. The relationships between these various forms of life, however, are complex: if the smaller species, dependent on the littoral, decline because of disruptions caused by the draw-down, there will be less food available for the pike and burbot and they, too, might decline. In some U.S. reservoirs pike have suffered because the spring draw-down has been as great as any other.

In general both the aquatic and terrestrial life in all its forms is already in a precarious state of equilibrium in this northern area, and our lack of knowledge about the ecosystem makes these species more vulnerable than they might otherwise be.

Downstream from the dams, the effects will also be great. The Nottaway and Broadback will be mere shadows of themselves in the lower 90 to 100 miles. First of all, most of the life in the Broadback riverbed will be swept away by the flooding from the Rupert diversions. Then the groundwater levels will be changed downstream, and there will probably be, as one man described it, "little deserts" where the rivers used to run, unless a series of small lakes are built to which the biota can adjust. Arctic char run up the Great Whale River: if its flow is reduced 50 percent they may not run up so far, and probably won't spawn. The effect of blocking the Caniapiscau (the task force bravely recommended against this) would be serious in Ungava Bay, an area of extremely high tides. The Caniapiscau is one of the great salmon rivers, and a 40 percent reduction in its level could be expected to wipe out its salmon entirely.

The behavior of sediments that are normally carried by the rivers into James Bay will be complicated by the impoundments. The original sediments will be dropped behind the dams, but this will increase the kinetic energy of the sediment-free waters, which can be expected in the early years to erode the downstream sections of the rivers and continue to carry sediments into James Bay. The effect on the bay is completely speculative. It is now in a state of equilibrium between these sediments and fresh waters, and the sea current and tides. The lower reaches of the La Grande are sandy and unstable, as is the Rupert River, the center of the NBR proposal. What seems certain is that there will be more erosion, which might prove extremely serious. In the last ten miles the Rupert River crosses the zone of clays of marine origin, and in 1969 a slide at mile three displaced 850,000 cubic yards of material — an indication of the instability of its banks. Some people expect unconsolidated deposits of sediments in Rupert Bay to be moved by the changes in currents caused by the diversions; one report suggests that the river mouth could be obstructed by extra deposits. Rupert House, which is built on a promontory, will become unstable in the future. This probability was known to the task force and was included in the first draft of its report, but was omitted from the final report, presumably so as not to let the Indians of Rupert House know what is likely to happen to their little village.

Dr. John Spence has pointed out that there are extensive beds of eel grass (*zostera marina*), the staple diet of brant geese, growing in Rupert Bay. It was once abundant along the eastern seaboard of the United States but began to disappear in 1932, and within a few years was almost completely gone, with a bad effect on geese and duck populations. Is this unhappy experience now to be repeated even in remote Rupert Bay? Most experts admit that the wildfowl habitat along the coast will be changed. Rupert Bay is crucial to the wildfowl migration. The early version of the ecological report (again the data was deleted from the final report) indicated that Rupert Bay has 4,500,000 geese-days of use in the spring (which presumably means either that a million geese stay there for 4½ days each, or four and a half million for a day) compared with only 12,500 in Fort George, located at the mouth of the La Grande. Rupert Bay has 6,000,000 geese-days of use in the autumn, compared with only 3,000 at the mouth of La Grande River. These figures indicate the enormous importance of this one small bay to North American wildfowl. Apart from the ecological importance of the wildfowl migration, the sports hunting of these birds in the United States is a $100,000,000 business. And it is of some importance in James Bay itself. In 1971 there were seventeen hunting camps there, of which eight were on the Quebec side. Some of these were run by the Department of Indian Affairs in collaboration with local Indians. The total number of birds taken in the whole bay was 27,800 for an estimated value of $1,123,000, of which about one-quarter went to the Indian camps.

Nobody knows, either, the effect of the proposed changes on the aquatic life in James Bay. J. Bryant, the director of the eastern region of the Canadian Wildlife Service, wrote the ecological task force that there are supposed to be several rare isolated forms of marine life in the bay that are not represented in Hudson Bay. He asked if adequate sampling had been carried out to ensure that the entire biota of the bay be known before any changes were made. He said, also, that some of the James Bay islands represented the southernmost extension of arctic tundra in eastern Canada, and suggested that weather changes might damage or destroy these plant communities. He said that the Twin Islands in James Bay, which appear to have been formed by the action of currents and tides, are an important area of polar bear activity, and asked if there was any danger they might be deformed or destroyed by changes in currents, tides and ice conditions created by the river changes. Bryant did not receive an answer from the task force. Similarly, one can only guess as to whether the changes will affect the beluga (or white whale), the bearded seal and the ringed seal in James Bay. These mammals feed largely on benthic fish, crustacea and mollusks, and it is conceivable that the change in the in-flow of nutrients could deplete these bottom-dwelling populations, and therefore also deplete the larger aquatic animals.

The effect which has given rise to more public discussion and argument than any other is that on the weather — possibly because it is the only effect to which city dwellers can relate. Here again, Russian scientists have been busy where Canadians have not. They have defined two zones of weather influence caused by water impoundments. The first of these occurs within ten kilometres of the lake; it can suffer a variation of annual temperature of from .5 to $1.5\,^\circ$C. The other occurs within 30 to 50 kilometres of the lake. There the variations are smaller, perhaps as low as $.3\,^\circ$ C. It is generally agreed that the factor most affected by water impoundments is wind, which can be increased by an artificial reservoir to an extent noticeable ten or fifteen miles away. When the lake is not frozen the average temperatures are a little warmer than usual in spring and autumn and colder over the whole year. In warm sunny weather the Russians have found that the air can be 3^0 colder above an artificial lake at 15 metres, and 2^0 at 30 metres. These effects are not unlike those of natural lakes. The Great Lakes, for example, are estimated to cause 50 percent of the snow that falls before freeze-up each autumn; similar, but local, effects are expected from the many big reservoirs being built in James Bay. The major climatic effects will be caused by the changes brought about in the ice regime of James and Hudson bays as a result of the regulation of the rivers. Just how big these effects are likely to be is not clear, though the ecological task force decided they would have only local effects. An interesting controversy on the subject was sparked during 1971 by Dr. L.H. Dickie, director of the Marine Ecology Laboratory at the Bedford Institute, Halifax. Very large quantities of fresh water pour into James Bay now. Dickie pointed out that in Hudson Bay the fresh-water outflow is mainly responsible for initiating the breakup of sea ice. Once it creates sufficiently large ice-free areas, this water becomes further mixed by wind action, and this also hastens the breakup by allowing the water to absorb heat from the sun and warm up quickly. Any reduction in spring flow, argued Dickie, would delay the onset of spring breakup, which would result in a longer winter. The effects, indeed, would be even greater. If river regulation delayed the autumn freeze-up, it would in turn tend to increase the early winter snowfall, since evaporation would be greater without the ice cover. The Labrador current is made up of 50 percent of surface water flowing out of Hudson Strait, and alterations in its structure and heat content could affect the climate of the entire East Coast. Wrote Dr. Dickie in May, 1971:

Effects of this sort are so large as to boggle the imagination. In fact they are so difficult to appreciate that they invite our disbelief. Because of their complexity the scientists cannot yet predict the aggregate effects in any detail.

We suggest that cost-benefit studies of such power developments as the one in question should take into account the indirect costs of possible ecological and climatological effects. The installation of these hydro-electric generating plants is not necessarily irrevocable. Thus if it were found sometime in the future that deterioration of climate had occurred to the significant detriment of forest and agricultural resources, or had resulted in an important proportion of the new power supply being offset by the power required for extra heat in homes and industries, the rivers could be restored to their normal flow patterns.

He concluded that these factors were so important that the minister for the environment and the minister of mines, energy and resources should be made aware of them.

By November, however, Dr. Dickie's team was reporting, "It is difficult to see a major change of far-reaching effect as a result of controlling the freshwater outflow from the NBR, or from the La Grande. By themselves the proposed changes are a very few thousand cubic feet per second less in spring for a short time and actually more for much of the year." They warned that a series of such systems around the shores of Hudson and James bays would no doubt have an effect on currents and climate.

The possibility that the heavy bodies of water imposed on a fairly unstable soil might cause earthquakes was dismissed by the ecological task force with the offhand statement that, though there have been some minor earthquakes in the region, the reservoirs will be shallow and the additional pressure so small that the danger of inducing earthquakes seems "definitely remote." Considerable detail given in the first draft of the report was omitted. The first draft, though it came to the same conclusion, had said the enormous quantities of water to be accumulated "could cause a certain uneasiness as to the unbalancing of the earth's surface." The thirty- or forty-foot depth of the reservoirs would add 17.5 pounds pressure per square inch. It noted that Manic 5 reservoir was ten times deeper and had so far recorded no bad effects. (Could this be because no readings have been taken — before, during or after impoundment?) Between 1928 and 1959 in eastern Canada some 391 earthquakes were recorded. On June 8, 1941, a quake which reached five on the Richter scale was recorded with an epicentre 125 miles east of James Bay and north of the Eastmain. A seismological station in operation on the Great Whale River since September, 1965, has recorded four minor earth tremors. Three of these were centred near Moosonee, on the Ontario side of the Bay, and one between Fort George and the Eastmain River. James Bay is shown on seismic maps as a no-damage zone, while most of the project area is shown as a minor damage zone. In general the task force's conclusion was that it was unusual for an earthquake to be centred on the Canadian shield, and it believed there was unlikely to be any risk of quakes caused by the weights of water involved.

W.K. Gummer, of the Bedford Institute, has seemed a little less confident. Although there was no relationship established in the Canadian experience between earthquakes and reservoirs, or between earthquakes and sensitive clay slides, nevertheless the supersaturated conditions preceding clay slides make it seem that an earth tremor could be proficient in triggering such slides, and "since sensitive clays occur in the James Bay sector there must be awareness of this possibility." This possibility has aroused fairly wide interest because the clays in the area are similar to those that slid disastrously in 1971 at St. Jean Vianney, a small town in the Lake St. Jean region to the east, causing many deaths. Engineers point out that the presence of such soils simply means that design must take account of these dangers. Safeguards are therefore built into the design at considerable extra cost — ones which were not taken into account when the decision to establish a town at St. Jean Vianney was made. This has implications not only for the cost of the project, but also for the cost of the power delivered to Montreal or New York. It was obvious at a very late stage that detailed design on which accurate cost estimates could be based had not yet been done, despite the confident statements a year before about how much the power was likely to cost.

Finally, the variety and beauty of the area are going to be drastically modified by the James Bay scheme. Most official reports suggest that the ugly scars be hidden from the public (shades of open-pit coal mining in the Rockies), and that dead trees be cut around the edges of any lakes where roads will run close by. But this is merely an example of the lip-service to multiple use that pervades the scheme. The ecological report expresses a great deal of enthusiasm about the great tourist potential of the area. Tourism is mentioned as a resource almost second to hydroelectricity; one remarkable passage states "the development of the NBR project would maximize the tourist development potential in terms of quality, quantity and variety."

How this conclusion is reached is unclear, for the only

appraisal of the tourist potential which apparently reached the task force arrived at exactly the opposite conclusion. It was written by M.R. Hargrave of the Canada Land Inventory in the Department of the Environment. "Unlike some hydroelectric developments such as the South Saskatchewan River project where the resulting reservoir produced a net gain with regard to outdoor recreation potential, the James Bay project will not," Hargrave wrote. "Already there is ample water in both regions. The effect would be rather a net loss in that lengthy sections of river valleys will be flooded, thus reducing the variety of water forms found within either region." The main benefit would come from "opening up large areas" for outdoor recreation. Mr. Hargrave said the proposed road into the north would be the deepest road incursion in Canada east of the Mackenzie Highway, but according to a judgment made of eight different factors, such as vegetation, water quality, river courses and so on, the La Grande River was more interesting from the tourist point of view. "It would be a mistake to anticipate a tourist boom to follow in the wake of the James Bay project," Mr. Hargrave added. And nobody has mentioned that black flies and mosquitoes, already a great deterrent to the white tourist, will be significantly increased. Hargrave's opinion did not appear in even the first draft report.

All of these factors, then, were evidently unknown or unregarded when Bourassa made the decision to proceed with the project. It is bitterly ironical that so irrational a decision was made in so precipitate a way by the first Quebec Cabinet ever to have been highly educated in the ways of the modern, technological world. Eighteen of the twenty-one members are university graduates — so different from the members of the old Quebec Cabinets, who had one foot in North America and the other somewhere in the last century.

Official government publications are just dripping with the implication that the land is lying up there, silent, waiting for the day when its lover will arrive from the south to tickle it into action with a clash of bulldozer gears. And empty, of course. "A wild and sterile area, from the point of view of use," said one report, "accessible only to some privileged people who can afford to hire a plane to go there." — What, no Indians? And when someone suggested that the project might change the climate, Bourassa is reported to have remarked, "Then people can wear an extra sweater."

Note For Chapter V:
1. In "Ecological Considerations of the James Bay Project," a report drawn up by Dr. John Spence and his wife Jill of the McGill University Department of Biology.

6. The International Experience

In almost every part of the world it has become commonplace for engineers to dream up huge schemes, and politicians to decide to implement them, long before the full consequences of the schemes have been studied in any detail. In that sense the James Bay project is heir to a growing, ignoble tradition. The creation of man-made lakes and the control of natural water bodies has reached such a scale that it can now be said these huge engineering works are modifying and changing the landscape of the earth more than either agricultural or urban expansion. [1]

The international record is rather a sorry one, for despite all our technical knowledge and engineering skill, the great man-made lakes that transformed many nations in the sixties were forced on at such speed that there is hardly one that has not caused serious, unforeseen side effects. Some of these side effects have been so severe as almost to nullify the advantages the lakes were supposed to create. Scientists from many disciplines have then been called in to study the effects, after the fact. The protection of the environment in the total sense has always been given low priority by those people concerned with creating the lakes. The international scientific community has gone through a kind of hand-wringing phase, the meaning of which boils down to an anguished plea to be consulted in the future during the *first* stages of planning.

It is estimated that only about 15 percent of all the man-made lakes created up to 1953 in the United States, the world's most technically advanced country, were planned in a satisfactory way. The preparations for the other 85 percent were inadequate by almost any standards.[2] But it does not appear that many lessons have been learned from these early disastrous experiences. Most of the biggest man-made lakes have been created since the early sixties, but the same blinkered vision has been brought to nearly all of the projects. Only fairly recently, in fact, have people begun to think of the study of man-made lakes as a science. When they did, they discovered that little data had been collected. Such data always referred to the dams which formed the lakes — a revealing bias which arose out of the engineering obsessions of our time. The only factor of interest to the dambuilder is storage capacity. So when the international register of dams was drawn up in 1964, the height, length, volume of the dam, and the storage capacity behind each dam were the only pieces of information included. The surface of the lakes, the lengths of shoreline, and their maximum and mean average depth were not stated.

In 1970 two German researchers[3] estimated that the world's man-made lakes covered 300,000 square kilometres (an area 20 percent bigger than the Great

Lakes) and had a storage capacity of about 4,000 cubic kilometres of water, or nearly one-third the total water content of the atmosphere. Their list of forty-one man-made lakes measuring more than 1,000 square kilometres each showed that only one such huge lake had been created in the world before World War II, and that was Gouin Reservoir on the St. Maurice River, not far south of the James Bay project. The extent to which the huge man-made lake is a modern phenomenon is indicated by twenty-nine of these lakes having been created since 1960 (eight in Canada, eighteen in the Soviet Union, and seven in Africa). Of the eleven measuring more than 4,000 square kilometres each, eight were built during the sixties.

The damming of rivers in the United States has gone so far that, according to one authority,[4] "scientists are now denied the opportunity of becoming acquainted with a really large temperate river that is not regulated in some manner." He adds that unaffected rivers still flow in arctic and tropical regions, but their remoteness would keep scientists from them about as long as dam builders — a prophecy that the James Bay project fulfills exactly.

Every man-made lake has been created for the benefit of mankind, either to produce electricity, or to prevent floods, or to store water for irrigation. Yet it is amazing that so many factors have been ignored when the experts were thinking about the effect the great dams would have and the way the bodies of water would behave. The more spectacular deleterious effects have taken place in tropical countries. It is true that few such spectacular effects are likely to be repeated in an area of intense cold such as James Bay. Nevertheless, it is worth examining the results of these other great interventions because they have all been embarked on, like the James Bay project, with the blithe confidence that everything would turn out well.

In Canada, as elsewhere, no attention has ever been paid to the ecological effects of diversion and impoundment schemes. Gouin Reservoir is a case in point. Though it is now more than sixty years since the reservoir was created, no serious studies have ever been undertaken of the effects of this impoundment. Nothing is known about Manicouagan, either, a reservoir in operation only since 1969. A 1964 Hydro-Quebec book about the wonders of the Manic dam is a classic example of blinkered engineering vision: it makes no reference of any kind to the environment, to the aquatic and terrestrial plant and animal life, or to the qualities of the impounded water. These were subjects which just did not occur to the engineering mind.

Similarly, Canada created an environmental disaster in British Columbia when the Bennett Dam was built on the Peace River. It so lowered the water levels several miles downstream in the Peace-Athabaska delta that hundreds of Indian and Métis trappers, their livelihoods shattered, were forced onto welfare. Additionally, it has been reported that engineering works have been necessary many hundreds of miles away, in the Mackenzie delta, because of the drop in water levels there, also caused by the Bennett Dam. When an industrialized nation with a strong scientific community and a powerful governmental structure shows so little concern for the wider issues involved in engineering works, it is not surprising that even more horrendous mistakes have been made in underdeveloped countries with almost non-existent research capacities.

It is interesting that the same criteria have always dominated these decisions. The same short-term motives that made Bourassa twist the arm of the Hydro-Quebec president have dictated hurried decisions about dam building in poorer countries. Everywhere, biologists and other scientists concerned with the totality of food chains and life cycles have been called in too late, as an afterthought — sometimes to deal with serious unforeseen problems, and sometimes (as in James Bay) to lend a spurious scientific respectability to a precipitate action. "In the planning phase," said Sir Robert Jackson, in a paper to a 1971 international symposium on man-made lakes, "all the factors influencing the project may be thoroughly, taken into account. That phase is naturally followed by one in which the government considers the project as a matter of policy and decides whether to go ahead or not." He is, naturally, describing the course to be followed by any government that had researched international experience with man-made lakes and tried to make rational decisions. It can be seen from his description that the Quebec government is not one of them because it made the decision to go ahead long before the planning phase even began. Jackson's second phase is that of decision making, followed by the third phase, mobilizing the finance, and the fourth, actual construction. Bourassa's method seems to have been unique: decision, construction, planning and financing, in that strange order.

The recorded international experience has brought scientists almost unanimously to the conclusion that ecologists, climatologists, biologists, sociologists and other specialists should be involved in field work before the construction of man-made lakes so they can participate in the decision making when the feasibility of river regulation is being discussed.[5] Experience has shown a wide range of ecological changes caused by river diversions and impoundments. Some of these were outlined by UNESCO consultants John E. Bardach, of the University of Michigan, and Bernard Dussart, of the Musée d'Histoire Naturelle of Paris, to the 1971 symposium. They included many effects that will undoubtedly be involved in the James Bay diversions. Included in their list were climatic changes, about which not enough hard data is yet available to make any generalizations possible. They suggested that in the future mankind may find it necessary to use great man-made lakes to lower temperatures as a means of offsetting the consequences of heat production caused by man in his restless search for energy. Great climatic changes could be caused by some of the bigger ideas that are still no more than beams in the eyes of engineers. One is a scheme to block off the Ob and Yenisei rivers in Siberia, and thus create an inland sea the size of Italy. There are schemes for damming the Amazon and creating an inland sea one-third the size of France. There is a scheme to let the Mediterranean into the Sahara and create a sea which will occupy 10 percent of the African continent. Such schemes would undoubtedly have a major modifying effect on climate. But so far few hard facts are known about the climatic effects of interventions that have already been made.

One major effect of man-made lakes is that sediment carried by the rivers is deposited behind the dams. This affects the productivity of the rivers downstream; the losses of these sediments on the flood plains and deltas of major rivers have been disastrous. Major changes in plant cover have occurred following all impoundments. Low-lying soils and plant associations change a lot. Some species disappear; others spread. Almost no studies of these likely effects have ever been made in advance of impoundment. The effect on birds and mammals has always been considerable. The impounded waters can increase carrying capacities by providing new nesting, feeding and watering opportunities, but on the other hand they flood much wildlife habitat. The key question here is the frequency and size of the water level fluctuations. Reservoir operations designed for other purposes, such as clearing out weeds, mosquito control, or irrigation, can come at a bad time for birds and animals, and destroy their feeding grounds. In a paragraph which could apply directly to James Bay, Bardach and Dussart said:

Large, deep man-made lakes can reduce the area of wildlife habitat in their watershed. The best niches for wildlife usually exist along river courses, and most species of large and small game have territories, home ranges and feeding circuits associated with the mainstream and/or its tributaries.

These will disappear in the flooded area. As the animals' behavior traits make them cling tenaciously to their home grounds, the arrival of the water spells death for most terrestrial creatures.

They said that decisions to build man-made lakes so that protein can be obtained from increased fish catches often overlook the possibility of harvesting wild game that would be destroyed by the flooding; and give as an example the prospect that fish protein derived from the planned lake to be created on the Mekong would probably not be any more valuable than would game farming of the dense concentration of ungulates which will probably be wiped out by the flooding.

The effect of man-made lakes on aquatic biota is also considerable. The changes sometimes afford the possibility of new fisheries by encouraging new species. By blocking fish runs, on the other hand, dams can also minimize fisheries. The initial flooding of plant life usually leads to proliferation of bacteria and depletion of oxygen, but later the oxygen content usually rises. The action of winds then tends to distribute the oxygen more evenly to counterbalance the effects of organic decomposition. This results in high productivity (which can mean a high fish catch in the early years after impoundment), but it later declines. These interactions between the various types of life behind a dam have not been very intensively studied. Nevertheless, it is established that a big river and its tributaries usually provide a more varied habitat than a lake, in which the number of species often diminishes. Some of the known interactions are fascinating: when the Kentucky Reservoir on the Tennessee River was closed off, the number of mussel species in the river was cut by half. A species that had been supporting a thriving button trade and providing Japan with inserts for cultured pearl production was eradicated. Sometimes, as in certain Mekong reservoirs, plankton production will explode. If there were no plankton feeders in the preimpounded waters, they must be introduced to take advantage of the food.

Normally after three or four years of high fish production the catch declines sharply and the decline may last for twenty years or more, as was confirmed for far-northern lakes by Swedish research into the effect of impoundments on bottom animals used as fish food.[6] The Russian I.I. Lapisky[7] says that the depression in productivity of a reservoir north of 50 degrees (the James Bay area lies just north of that latitude) may last twenty-five to thirty years. After that some recovery can be expected. Bardach and Dussart said that though much ingenuity has gone into development of fish ladders and other devices to circumnavigate man-made barriers, "they still leave much to be desired." They concluded: "Detailed fishery biology investigations over many years prior to dam building are indicated if direct fish gains from man-made lakes are to be weighed against the possible fish losses of constructing a barrage in the river."

One element not likely to be present in James Bay is the creation of disease. In tropical countries this has been a major disadvantage of man-made lakes. But there is no doubt that many man-made lakes have caused mental and emotional disturbances, and this could well happen to the Indians in James Bay. It is well documented now that one way to destroy a people and a culture is to make it clear to them that they cannot control the decisions governing their own lives. A danger which might befall a decision by the Cree people to fight the James Bay project is for them, in the end, to have their morale broken by knowledge of their lack of power. Bardach and Dussart concluded their paper by saying:

Ecologists have often stressed the value of biotic diversity. Unmodified ecosystems are usually more diverse and resilient than man-dominated ones. Perhaps planning ought to include options of minimum as opposed to massive interference in ecosystem balance. The application of the systems approach to the planning and management of man-made lakes is clearly indicated, but this can only be effective if the data fed into such analyses are adequate.

To date inputs to the planning and cost accounting of man-made lakes have been slanted in favor of the more easily quantifiable consequences often computed in a random and piecemeal fashion. In order not to repeat costly schemes that are eventually abandoned, or whose benefits prove to be far less than anticipated, it is imperative to make provision for early and intensive field work by ecologists prior

to the construction of man-made lakes, and to ensure the participation of ecologists in the planning
and decision-making counsels that consider the
feasibility of river regulation.

Many of the factors they mentioned will apply in the
James Bay diversions, and one that is especially ap-
plicable is that none of the really necessary ecological
work has been done in James Bay any more than it was
done in any of the other engineering schemes.

The scale of the interventions now being made in
natural river systems is indicated by the following facts:
the annual runoff of water in the world is 37,000 cubic
kilometres. The proportion stored naturally is 33 percent; it will be increased to 67 percent through human
intervention by the year 2000.[8] In the long-term this is
expected to reduce by 3 to 5 percent the total runoff
because of the expected increase in evaporation from
these storage basins.

The low priority given to biologists, ecologists,
sociologists and others concerned with human and
natural systems is indicated by the history of some of the
lakes created in recent years.

Preparatory work on the *Aswan* dam was completed in
1955 and the first Russian loan was negotiated in 1958.
Yet the social survey of the people to be moved by the
dam was not done until 1960, and comprehensive plans
for them not drawn up until 1962 — seven years after
construction had started. The dam was designed to bring
two million acres of land under cultivation through
irrigation and to produce electricity. But for some reason
the Nile deposition of 134 million tons of fertile silt
downstream was overlooked. With the loss of this silt,
agriculture can be kept going only by importation of artificial fertilizers. Furthermore, the blocking of water-
borne nutrients has robbed sardines in the

Mediterranean of their food and reduced the average catch from 18,000 tons to 500 tons a year, a loss which the additional catch of 4,500 tons of fish in the lake behind the dam has not offset. Financially, the loss is estimated at about $7 million annually. The loss of silt has also resulted in serious erosion of the shoreline of the sea. As explained by John P. Milton, acting director of the international program section of the Conservation Foundation in Washington, D.C.[9]: "The delta of the Nile was in a delicate equilibrium between the rate of erosion from the Mediterranean and the rate of deposition provided by the silt which was annually deposited. The problem was that when the High Aswan was constructed, it immediately began to trap the same sediment, which was no longer available for deposition in the delta, and the rate of erosion from the Mediterranean took precedence and dominated." (This could happen in Rupert Bay.) To correct the shoreline erosion, the Egyptian government now has to spend $250 million on a series of ten dams between the High Aswan and the sea, designed to slow down the siltfree water.

Though the dam has added $500 million a year to the Egyptian national income, the cost of bilharzia, the terrible disease that is spreading rapidly through the tropical world in the wake of diverted and mandominated waters, is likely to rise to $100 million a year, according to estimates by Bardach and Dussart. Bilharzia (known outside Africa as schistosomiasis) is caused by a fork-tailed worm that develops on snails in water. It attaches itself to anyone who enters the water, enters his blood stream, and lays its eggs there. The eggs are then excreted into water where they develop into larvae that enter more snails. The disease was present to an unknown extent before the damming of the Nile, but when irrigation schemes are complete it is expected to have infected 50 percent of Egypt's rural population. It causes lassitude and could result in a 30 to 50 percent reduction in a male worker's production. Another negative factor from the damming is that evaporation is so great in the hot desert country that some authorities expect less water to be available for irrigation in the future than before the dam was built. [10] Dr. A.A. Ahmed, former chairman of the Egyptian Hydro-Electric Power Commission, in 1960 — too late, again — suggested that a better scheme would have been to divert Nile waters for storage into a nearby natural basin, the Wadi Rayan depression. He has said, [11] "Evaporation losses appear to be so great as to make the High Dam of doubtful benefit, if not hazardous." Some 120,000 people were displaced by the Aswan Dam.

Behind the *Volta* Dam in Ghana lies the world's biggest man-made lake — 3,275 square miles in area — occupying 4 percent of Ghana's land surface. The idea for such a lake was first studied in 1952, work was started in September, 1961 and the lake began to fill in May, 1964. Two million acres were to be flooded where 80,000 people, or 1 percent of Ghana's population, lived in 750 villages. They were mostly subsistence farmers dwelling in mud huts with thatched roofs. By the end of 1964, 55,000 of them had been flooded out and evacuated. In 1965 research was recognized as an essential part of the lake management, and in 1968 the Volta Lake Research Project was launched. The attempt to survey the land to be flooded and plan facilities for those evacuated did not begin until 1962. The plan was to move them into fifty-two villages, to clear thousands of acres for them and set them up in mechanized and modernized farms. Yet it was not until 1968 that the method of land ownership was determined, so only 8,000 acres were cleared and ready for the new settlers when they were moved out of their old villages.[12] Sixty percent of the original resettled people moved away from the area; some 60,000 Ewe farmers moved to the shores of the lake to become fishermen. They set themselves up in about a thousand villages, completely unserviced, hidden in the trees along the edge of the lake. Only when it was decided to make 438,000 acres available for subsistence farming in two-to-four-acre plots did the original inhabitants begin to move back.

The people living on the shores initiated a form of agriculture the authorities hadn't thought of: they began to grow tomatoes, okra, peppers, maize, groundnuts and even rice in the 200 yards of the shoreline exposed by a lake draw-down of ten feet. This sort of agriculture has such potential that it is estimated it could produce rice equivalent to 30 percent of the present imports. Because it was essential to produce electricity for the aluminum industry at a rate competitive with world prices, it was not possible to spend money on clearing dead trees from the bottom of the lake. Therefore, there were plenty of nutrients available when the lake was newly flooded. Fish became plentiful and by 1969 the catch was estimated at 60,000 metric tons. But by 1970 it had fallen to 38,000 tons. The soft parts of the trees had already decomposed, but the cores of the trees were expected to take decades to rot. The problem, then, was to find some way to enrich the bottom of the lake enough to support the lowest elements in the food chain, on which so much depended. "A decline in fish production is a serious matter," says Dr. Letitia Obeng, director of Ghana's Institute for Aquatic Biology.[13] "Preventing a continuous decline is vital. Replacing and maintaining a satisfactory level of nutrient material appears difficult, but it is important and should receive urgent attention."

The lake has caused health problems, too. During 1968 and 1969 bilharzia was transmitted on a high level, and it was estimated that in some places where only two years before only 10 percent of the children had the disease, the rate of infection had reached almost 100 percent. In 1970 the rate of infection began to fall, possibly, according to E.A.K. Kalitsi, director of finance for the Volta River Authority,[14] because the fish stocks approached nearly to equilibrium with the aquatic weed on which the snails feed. This is a peculiarly fascinating example of the delicate balance of nature — the snails and the fish are in competition for the same food. Man gets food from fish and disease from snails. The balance between fish and fish-food therefore is a vital question for the area's inhabitants.

The breeding places of the black fly that is the vector of river blindness were wiped out by the lake but the incidence of this disease increased downstream at the rapids. According to different estimates, 50 percent of the people over forty who live on the lake are blind, while 90 percent of the people downstream over fifteen are blind.[15] The weeds that provide good habitat for the mosquito carrying yellow fever and the snail carrying bilharzia have spread over part of the lake, yet by 1971 no effective control measures had been found. "Volta Lake has created new production opportunities," Kalitsi says, "but we have not been able to exploit the new opportunities open to us." Although the essence of the project was to provide people with improved living conditions and the necessary incentive for productive effort, in practice, "the people could not even operate at their old production possibilities level, and development was clearly hampered by the tension of displacement and unrealized expectations."

Advance investigations into the possible effects of the

Kariba Dam on the Zambesi were a little more effective than in most other large schemes. The dam was finished in December, 1958, but studies of the fish populations in the river had been made by a Joint Fisheries Research Organization in 1956 and 1957, 50,000 people were moved by 1958, and limnology, plant life, seismic movement and fisheries were studied from a fairly early stage in the history of the new lake. Yet even this record of concern is not regarded by all authorities as exemplary. Ecologist Thayer Scudder[16] of the California Institute of Technology points out that little interest was taken in the lake until events there threatened operations at the dam. The Kariba Lake Coordinating Committee was organized and held its first meeting two years after the 1955 decision to build, and was given tasks connected with establishing a fishery on the lake. Its budget dwindled until it was disbanded. There followed a proliferation of ill-organized bodies concerned with development of the lake. (Prof. Scudder comments that in dam-building projects a national committee with a strong research orientation is absolutely essential "since it would at least increase the chance of a well-planned research program being initiated prior to the creation of new lakes.")

All the effort at Kariba did not prevent a major problem — the spreading over 15 percent of the lake's surface of a plant called *salvinia auriculata*, which had first appeared in the lake in 1959. Chemical means of control were found to be prohibitively expensive, so biological means were being considered in 1971. As for other problems, despite the preparation, fish catches have not reached the level forecast. Estimates of the likely catch ranged from 10,000 to 31,000 tons a year; the actual catch reached about 6,000 tons in 1964, but had declined to less than half that by 1969. The bilharzia snail increased from 1964, and heavy infestations of local people were reported by 1967.

Additionally, Kariba illustrates another unknown factor in the creation of enormous man-made lakes — the danger of earthquakes.[17] The area was almost seismically inert before the lake was formed. Then in 1959 shocks were measured when the water level had risen to sixty metres. Crustal depression was measured thirty-six kilometres from the lake; it was suggested that it was a result of elastic bending of the strata, caused by the weight of water on the land. Weak seismic activity culminated in 1963-64 in short-lived bursts which measured six on the Richter scale, the first time a shock of such magnitude had been artificially created. By 1971 scientists believed the area was settling down. Gordon Rattray-Taylor[18] points out that similar hopes had been expressed in 1967 about the Koyna Dam in India, which imposed a weight of two billion tons of water on the land — which, it is now agreed, caused severe earthquakes in December, 1967, and killed 200 people. Lake Mead in the United States also has had a seismic history. The water there weighs 25 billion tons; thousands of tremors were registered in ten years,[19] the strongest being five on the Richter scale. These shocks are believed to have been caused by the overload of Lake Mead water reactivating faults that had been stable since the Pleistocene era. Also in the United States, the Tennessee Valley system, while causing enormous industrial development along the banks of rivers, has had to face almost all the problems outlined here, including enormous weed growth.

Earthquake shocks have been caused by artificial lakes in four U.S. states, and in France, Italy, Pakistan, India, Spain, Algeria, Switzerland, Zambia and Greece.[20] Rattray-Taylor comments: "The imagination boggles at the probable effect of the great inland seas such as the Amazon, with its 170 billion tons of water." M.I. Van der Lingen, of the Department of National Parks and Wildlife Management in Rhodesia,[21] concluded his summary of the case history of Lake Kariba for the international symposium by saying: "Some natural processes appear to have been telescoped within a short period in the evolution of man-made lakes. It is important to understand these changes thoroughly before greatly interfering with the system, and as the study of man-made lakes progresses a firmer understanding of the basic principles will be obtained, allowing for wiser interference than perhaps has previously been the case."

A similar case history of *Brokopondo* Lake on the Suriname River in Dutch Guiana (Surinam) in South America, given to the same international meeting, led P. Leentvaar of the State Institute for Nature Management in Holland inexorably to the same conclusion: "In the planning of dams, biological knowledge should be included. If we had known before the construction of the dam what a unique river the Suriname was, we might have given some push for the location of the dam in another, biologically less valid region." Like James Bay, Brokopondo was built in a wilderness, far from anywhere, inhabited only by 5,000 Bush Negroes who were moved away. It was built only to supply electricity for an aluminum works and has created such a mess of half-drowned trees and endless lake peripheries that the lake is useless for any other purpose. After impoundment, water hyacinth spread quickly over the surface of the lake, from 5,000 hectares in 1964 to 41,200 hectares in 1966. Almost nothing was known beforehand about the biology of the area — for example, previously unknown plants, animals and fish were identified during postimpoundment studies — and the lake took far longer to fill than had been expected, because of evapotranspiration through the mat of water hyacinth. Fish fauna in the lake immediately became very poor compared with that in other parts of the river and other river systems. Leentvaar concluded: "In the pre-impoundment phase of damming plans, a long period of research into the flora and fauna of the region should be made. It is of the highest importance that all knowledge is used before any attack is made on our environment."

These failures have been described not for the sake of repeating many environmental horror stories, but to show that few lessons have been learned, and that Bourassa's decision about James Bay is an absolutely classic example of the sort of mistake continuing to cause serious problems in many countries around the world. In one country after another, authorities are pressing forward with schemes conceived for a single short-term purpose — flood control, irrigation or electrical production — that will have ramifications which the people responsible for the decisions have not bothered to take into account. The state of Florida is a prime laboratory example of man's appalling rape of natural systems for short-term gain. [22] In the Ivory Coast the government plans to move 85,000 people to make way for the new Lake Kossue in the Bandama Valley. The people will move into a crowded environment which will provide ideal conditions for the communication of diseases, so doctors are predicting an increase in river blindness (which already stands at 15 percent), sleeping sickness, paralytic poliomyelitis, intestinal infections and bilharzia, not to mention severe psychological disruption likely to be caused by a move into a different type of habitat. [23] Yet the Ivory Coast government boasts proudly about the project. The Lower Mekong in Indochina supports 20 million people from a huge fishery, and seven existing impoundments indicate that the catch can be increased. And therefore, the government is now considering building five new dams on the main river, ten on tributaries and eighteen other possible dam sites.[24] These schemes would flatten out waters in which all the aquatic life is adjusted — as in James Bay — to violent seasonal flooding, in this case from the monsoon. There is little information available about the biology of the Mekong fishes, and no one really knows whether these schemes will improve things or worsen them. In Zambia electricity from the Kariba is already inadequate to meet demand, and there is a scheme afoot to provide more by building a small dam at the top of a gorge on the Kafue River as it falls down to the Zambesi. The shallow lake behind this dam would cover 1,200 square miles, control the normal flooding of the Kafue flats, modify the vegetation and affect a 6,000-ton-a-year fishery as well as the range of 240,000 cattle and uncounted wild game.[25]

"Biological problems involve so many variables," wrote R.H. Lowe-McConnell of England, in a summary of recent world experience with fisheries in man-made lakes,[26] "that getting answers to them generally takes longer than does finding answers to engineering questions, so biological surveys must be started in good time if they are to provide reliable indications of fish production. Fishery biologists need to be included in planning teams from an early stage, and to work closely with the engineers and others concerned with the project."

The distinguishing characteristic of all these great schemes, and of all this experience, is that it was undertaken in a flush of technological confidence which rested on undoubted engineering skills. As Canadians are becoming more and more aware, there are few construction projects imaginable today which cannot be carried out if society is prepared to ignore the subtle web of consequences and to invest enough of its money in them. Oil tankers can be sent around the Northwest Passage, and there are people with the inclination and the money to do it. Pipelines can be built in permafrost, and there are people anxious to do that. The North American Water and Power Alliance scheme emanating from the J.M. Parsons Company of Los Angeles shows that it would be feasible to reverse the Yukon and some of the other great Canadian rivers, turn the interior of British Columbia into a lake, and funnel the waters south to the arid parts of the United States. Some people in the United States really want to do that, and they do not know or care about the effect such water transfers would have on the Canadian north. Similarly, it is not only possible to dam the Nile, the Mekong, the Mississippi, but also to turn the Amazon basin into a sea and make the Sahara into a lake, and dam up most of the rivers of northern Quebec. But someone, somewhere, has to feel the responsibility for the consequences, if the governments and the engineers fail to do so.

The provisions under U.S. law for environmental impact reports at least lend some legal authority to those who do not wish to hand over all decision making to the engineers. In the States at least three years are considered necessary for actual preimpoundment surveys and related research, plus a minimum of two years for programming the work, for a total five-year lead time given to the biologists before design engineering is begun, according to one authority.[27] The Canadian safeguards are deficient in this respect. The development of resources is a provincial matter; no Canadian federal government has ever really tried to stop a provincial government from developing resources. There are certain acts which the federal government could use if it wished to block a province (though clearly the Trudeau government has no wish to embarrass the pro-federalist Bourassa government). The federal government could intervene under the Navigable Waters Protection Act, which provides that no work shall be built in a navigable water without the approval of the minister of transport. Navigable waters have in the past been freely interpreted to mean waters on which it was possible and customary to navigate even with a canoe. But in Canadian practice, interference with the James Bay project on such flimsy grounds would be regarded as unwarranted. Federal power under the Migratory Birds Convention Act is very much that of wildlife conservation, according to a legal opinion taken by the Sierra Club of Ontario, and wildlife will no doubt be affected by the James Bay project. Canada also has federal responsibility for the regulation of trade and commerce for the sea coast and inland fisheries, and for Indians and lands reserved for Indians. But a year after Bourassa's announcement no interventions had been made on any of these subjects. The most likely (and indeed, only inescapable) intervention at the federal level would be that on the part of the National Energy Board, which has the duty to licence all exportations of energy. On the whole, none of these powers seem sufficiently strong to stop a determined provincial government with the necessary financial backing. So federal action will probably depend on a political judgment of the advisability of the scheme.

The James Bay project has come to public prominence almost coincidentally with the establishment of the first federal Department of the Environment. The department immediately undertook three studies of the ecological impact of big schemes proposed in different parts of the country — the proposed Mackenzie Valley oil pipeline, the Ste. Scholastique airport near Montreal and the James Bay project. Despite the fair words spoken by federal politicians about their concern for the environment, both in relation to arctic development and James Bay, the results of these three interventions do not suggest that the federal government can be looked to as a staunch defender of the environment against the depredations of the industrialists and their development ethic. Jack Davis, as federal environment minister, may have said that whenever an alternate source of clean power is available at similar cost, the rule should be "Don't dam, don't flood, don't produce any water power at all," but when it comes to the point, his statement just doesn't seem to mean anything.

The trouble is that the federal and provincial governments share the development ethic with the businessmen who have their ear. A different set of values is needed. Early in 1971 Thomas F. Malone, dean of the graduate school at the University of Connecticut and vice-president of the International Council of Scientific Unions, told the dam builders [28] that when our improving understanding of the physical universe is placed in an environmental context, it can be seen that there are major inadequacies in our knowledge, our attitudes and our institutions. The constraints imposed by the limited abilities of the human mind and muscle have been lifted. Our responsibility for the spaceship earth is increasing with the growth in our ability to modify natural systems. Pollution, land use and resources are the critical problems for the next 100 years. Already changes in the physical features of the earth's surface have gone so far that "if further extended they will begin to approach the threshold of global significance." Temperatures already are higher over cities than over countryside, fog more frequent, cloud more prevalent, precipitation 5 to 10 percent higher, and windspeeds reduced by up to 25 percent. In short, a different set of values must animate our legislators. But the changes in values will not easily be arrived at, as the James Bay project shows. Economists and politicians are still wedded to what Kenneth Boulding[29] calls "the cowboy economy" in which there are supposed to be infinite pools from which resources can be obtained and into which effluence can be dumped, measured only by production and consumption. In contrast, Buckminster Fuller's idea of the closed system of the spaceship earth is gaining wide acceptance. This spaceship economy is "measured by the nature, distribution, quality and variety of the whole capital stock, including the physical and mental well being of all the people in the system."

About a year before Bourassa announced the James Bay project, a group of ecologists, architects and scientists who had studied the likely course of mid-northern Canadian development for the Mid-Canada Development Foundation wrote a report which might have been meant to apply to the James Bay project. The report was a strange accompaniment to that whole development-oriented Mid-Canada Corridor ripoff, and was not greeted with any enthusiasm by the industrialists who were lining up to take their share of the spoils.

"We recommend," the ecologists wrote, "initiation of a comprehensive development plan for Mid-Canada which gives priority to rigorous ecological restraints." These would include a long-range goal for a stable Canadian population, abandonment of the concept of waste disposal in favor of restrictions on production and consumption of some consumer goods, conservation of resources until a need is demonstrated, clearly defined and quantified environmental quality standards, consideration for human ecological factors (especially the interests of the indigenous population) and acceptance by developers that the onus is on them to ensure that no irreversible damage to the ecosystem will result from their proposals.

If any one of these suggestions had any influence with any level of Canadian government, the James Bay project would be a dead duck.

Notes For Chapter VI:

1: David W. Ehrenfeld, *Biological Conservation*, p. 30, Holt, Rinehart and Winston, 1971.

2: Sir Robert Jackson, United Nations Special Fund, paper to International Symposium on Man-Made Lakes, Tennessee, May, 1971.

3: E. Fels, Munich, and R. Keller, Freiburg, paper *World Register of Man-Made Lakes* to Tennessee symposium.

4: Joe Kendall Neel, chapter on Impact of Reservoirs, from *Limnology in North America*, University of Wisconsin Press.

5: The following summary of some of the major effects of diversions in international experience draws on the Bardach-Dussart paper to the Tennessee symposium.

6: Ulf Grimäs, "Effects of Impoundment on the Bottom Fauna of High Mountain Lakes," *Abstracts of Uppsala Dissertations in Science*. This is one of a series of papers on impounded waters roughly comparable to those of James Bay.

7: Quoted by W.C. Beckman, FAO, p.154, Man-Made Lakes, proceedings of a 1966 symposium, published jointly by the Institute of Biology and Academic Press.

8: Pierre Dumas, chef de vision, études speciales et recherches, service hydraulique, projets de centrales, Hydro-Quebec, unpublished report on the Tennessee symposium.

9: Quote by Darrell J. Turner, in article "Dams and Ecology," magazine *Civil Engineering*, September, 1971.

10: Gordon Rattray-Taylor, *Doomsday Book*.

11: Gordon Rattray-Taylor, *Doomsday Book*.

12: E.A.K. Kalitsi, director of finance, Volta River Authority, paper to Tennessee symposium.

13: Paper on Volta River research to Tennessee symposium.

14: Same as 12.

15: Stanley Johnson, article *The Ecologist*, Nov. 1971; Letitia Obeng, same as 13.

16: Appendix to *Man-Made Lakes, A Selected Guide to the Literature*, compiled by Africa Science Board in cooperation with African section of the Library of Congress.

17: M.I. Van der Lingen, Department of National Parks and Wildlife Management, Rhodesia, paper on Kariba Lake to Tennessee symposium.

18: *Doomsday Book*.

19: Dale Hoffman and Al R. Jonez, U.S. Department of the Interior, Bureau of Reclamation, paper on Lake Mead to Tennessee symposium.

20: Paper by H.K. Gupta, B.K. Rastogi and Hari Narain, *Common Features of Reservoir-Associated Seismicity*, to Tennessee symposium.

21: Same as 17.

22: Paper *Rise and Fall of Lake Apopka* by R.F. Schneider and J.A. Little, Federal Water Quality Administration, to Tennessee symposium.

23: B.B. Waddy, paper *Health Problems of Man-Made Lakes* to Tennessee symposium.

24: V.R. Pantulu, of Mekong Secretariat, paper *Fisheries Problems and Opportunities in the Mekong* to Tennessee symposium.

25: E. White, paper *Kafue Hydro-Electric Scheme and its Biological Problems* to Tennessee symposium.

26: Paper to Tennessee symposium.

27: Richard Stroud, p.206, *Man-Made Lakes*, proceedings of 1966 conference.

28: Paper *Environmental Context*, to Tennessee symposium.

29: In *Britain's Economic Prospects*, published by Allen and Unwin, quoted by Philip Brachi in article on Economics and Ecology, *The Ecologist*, November, 1971.

7. The Self-fulfilling Prophecy

Only two serious justifications for the James Bay project have ever been offered. One is that the province needs the electricity; the other that it needs the jobs that will be created. Most people take the second of these needs very seriously because Quebec has a chronic unemployment problem, worsened by the release to the labor market during the last few years, for the first time in the province's history, of a large pool of educated young people. Quebec is on the periphery of the Great Lakes megalopolis, and recently has not been able to match the economic growth of neighboring Ontario. Bourassa's concern for jobs, therefore, is understandable, and few people in the province doubt this is a correct priority.

But will the James Bay project create the jobs he claims for it? So far he has failed to convince many people, for the promised 125,000 jobs seems to be a figure literally plucked from the air. Unfortunately, at the same meeting at which he made that promise, he boasted that in his first year in office his government had created 188,000 jobs "directly and indirectly," a claim so wildly at variance with any of the known facts that no one has since been able to take his extravagant claims seriously. Editorialist Jean-Paul Desbiens, editor of Montreal's largest daily, *La Presse*, mockingly suggested that in this perspective one could perhaps be said to create three or four jobs indirectly by taking a plane to Paris.[1] By the end of the year Bourassa claimed that in 1971 his government had been able to create 55,000 jobs of the 100,000 he had promised during his election campaign. Even that seemed a pretty inflated figure — a suspicion confirmed when official government statistics in March, 1972, showed that in the twelve months before February, 1972, Quebec had created only 23,000 jobs.

Bourassa has a tendency, then, to exaggerate — his 188,000 figure seems likely to have been about an 800 percent exaggeration. So the 125,000 promised jobs from James Bay remain difficult to identify, even when one employs the multiplier, that seemingly endless chain of cause and effect by which any one new job is supposed to lead to three or four more, which presumably, will lead to others. Bourassa claimed that by 1978, 56,000 men would be working on construction in James Bay, a figure ten times greater than the maximum number employed at the highest point on the great Manicouagan 5 Dam. Churchill Falls in 1970 had 6,500 workers on the site, a figure which in 1971 dropped to about 4,500. The forest industry might provide some extra work, and the manufacture of the turbines, if done in Montreal, would maintain jobs for men who are now working on similar machinery for other power stations. The maximum figure of workers on the job forecast by the director of construction for Hydro-Quebec is for 21,000 in 1977. A 1969 report made by a consulting engineer on natural resources of northwest Quebec suggested that hydro development would employ only 4,000. Thus, Bourassa's figures are not even approached by any other forecaster. By June, 1972, the 56,000 jobs forecast had officially shrunk to about 12,000, for the La Grande version of the project.

Economist Jacques Parizeau, an important adviser to Quebec governments during the sixties until he threw in his lot with Lévesque's Parti Québecois, declared that the promise of 125,000 jobs was a mockery, and could only be approached if the multiplier effect of five or six was posited. [2] Since by the nature of the work this kind of multiplier would not apply, it was left to the government to explain how the Bourassa figure had been reached, something that a year later still had not been done. (A multiplier of 1.4 was used in one of the engineering studies.) Indeed, by that time it was becoming obvious that the 125,000 projection was perhaps an exaggeration by about 600 percent.

If Quebec has $6 billion or $10 billion to spend, is the James Bay project the most effective way of spending it? Until now the government has never tried to prove that case. So far as anyone can find out, no serious comparative studies were made before Bourassa's dramatic commitment to the project. (Indeed, such studies would have taken a considerable time.)

At first it was assumed that Bourassa must have found some of the money needed for this huge development during his peregrinations around the money halls of the world. Indeed, he gave the impression that some kind of deal had been made with Consolidated Edison in New York for it to become the main customer. It soon became clear that neither the financiers nor the customers had been found, and that the decision to go ahead had been made in spite of this minor oversight. When people asked where the money would come from, Bourassa said

Coom Coomishish and his wife: "We think of our grandchildren, that they should be able to hunt as well. We hope they will not drown the earth."

A native hunting camp may still be the best school in the world.

gaily, "The money will come from where the money is. I know what I am doing." As the months went by, more and more people began to wonder if he was not entirely out of his depth.

When David Rockefeller, of the Chase Manhattan Bank in New York, went to Montreal in March, 1972, he was full of praise for Bourassa but he was vague about James Bay. He was interested, of course, and his bank would give serious consideration to any proposal about James Bay that it might receive. But so far it had not received a proposal. At the same time Wall Street moneymen said it was simply too early to talk about it; the engineering studies would have to be done first. The Wall Street firm of Morgan, Stanley, who played a part in financing the Churchill Falls development, was admitted to the Montreal Stock Exchange, evidently with the idea of taking part in the James Bay financing. Hydro-Quebec in its financial prospectus at the beginning of February 1972, said it had deposited with the hydroelectric subsidiary of the James Bay Corporation (the James Bay Energy Corporation, of which Hydro-Quebec is 51 percent owner) a subscription for seven million shares of its capital stock for a price of $700 million spread over ten years. But this had been the only money offered so far. Expenditures of about $28 million were incurred by Hydro-Quebec on behalf of the James Bay Energy Corporation in 1971, said the prospectus. Furthermore, "Expenditures of about $110 million have been projected for 1972, principally for roads and installations. Capital expenditures to be incurred for the James Bay project cannot be estimated until the ultimate scope of the program and the sequence of development is established. Apart from its proposed subscription for shares in the James Bay Energy Corporation, the amount and form of the commission's financial participation in the project had not been determined." So all remained vague. Despite that, Bourassa said at the opening of the Quebec legislative session, "The James Bay development has been decided on irreversibly."

Since most of the money for financing would have to come from foreign sources, what would be the impact of this capital importation on the Canadian economy? Obviously, Bourassa had failed to clear his enthusiasm with the federal government before rushing into his announcement. For months the James Bay project was greeted in Ottawa with a pained silence because the federal government was in a difficult spot. It could not slap Bourassa down without weakening his position. And since he seemed to be the best hope in Quebec for a strong federalism to oppose the drift to separatism, Trudeau obviously felt he had to maintain a diplomatic silence, at least for the moment. Enough well-informed people were already hanging around in the wings ready to shoot down Bourassa. Only a few months before, Eric Kierans, one of Trudeau's Cabinet ministers and a former president of the Montreal Stock Exchange, had indiscreetly blurted out that his federal Cabinet colleagues who were begging the Americans to build a pipeline to carry Alaska oil down the Mackenzie Valley to middle western markets were asking for trouble. Such a pipeline, said Kierans, would cost $8 billion at least, and the importation of $8 billion into Canada would seriously undermine the strength of the Canadian dollar and destroy Canada's competitive position in world markets. Later Kierans had resigned from the Cabinet in protest against the federal government's policy of encouraging capital-intensive investment by an extensive system of write-offs and tax concessions, which, he said, were practically forcing American firms to buy out Canadians. He had embarked on a campaign to persuade young people up and down the country that Canada was the only country in the world forcing someone else to colonize it. And now he made no secret of the fact that the same arguments would apply to the James Bay financing, if it ever took place, and that Bourassa was making the same mistake the federal Cabinet had made with the pipeline. Instead of stalling the Americans and letting them discover their need for the pipeline, and for Canadian electricity, it was begging the Americans to come in by hook or by crook, thereby destroying the Canadian bargaining position. Consolidated Edison was no doubt interested in buying power, argued Kierans, but since Bourassa had already decided to build the project, the New York utility could afford to wait and see what happened.

During the months that followed, the justifications given for the James Bay project kept changing in a bewildering fashion. At one moment it was designed to save the American northeast from a crippling power shortage (at a handsome profit to Canadians); at the next, if Ottawa would invest in it, it would be a unique opportunity to strengthen Canada's economic independence.

"The Canadian government through the Bank of Canada might find it interesting to finance this project which could serve all Canada," said Bourassa in an interview nine months after his decision to go ahead. "It is an asset for Quebec and can become an asset for Canada. When you consider the whole problem of energy policies, the export of our natural resources, and the need to have some of our resources processed here, Quebec with this development has an advantage over Canada and the rest of North America." Two months later, however, the emphasis had changed again. By this time he had had his promised talk with Trudeau, and was no longer talking so optimistically about Ottawa support. "I discussed it in the following context," he told a questioner in the National Assembly. "If the Canadian government wanted to restrict the possibility of provinces borrowing on the foreign market, it should logically provide other solutions for the provinces such as the Bank of Canada. I think we have to borrow from outside in one form or another. As we do not have the Bank of Canada to finance our deficits, it is normal that those who could restrict Quebec's borrowing power or restrict our loan markets should provide us with other markets." No wonder Bourassa is so amenable to David Rockefeller, who in 1963 had tried to buy into Canadian banking,[3] and who took the opportunity again in 1972 to say that Canadian restrictions against foreign capital would be unwelcome to him. With friends like Bourassa in Canada, American capital can hardly go wrong.

Truly by this time James Bay was becoming all things to Bourassa. But economist Parizeau asked awkward questions, such as, how could Quebec carry the loan?[4] A $6-billion project supposes that the combined debt of the province and of Hydro-Quebec could be doubled. Already the province is borrowing $325 million a year, and Hydro-Quebec $300 million. Even if Hydro's current borrowing were reduced to $200 million, and the financing of the project spread over ten years, the utility would still be faced with borrowing $800 million annually for the next ten years (or if not Hydro-Quebec, then the James Bay Development Corporation, which would also require a provincial government guarantee). This would mean that the total borrowings of the government and Hydro-Quebec would be more than $1 billion a year, and Parizeau concluded, "There is just no realism in this" because the Quebec government recently has had difficulty raising $600 million a year. The force of his argument seemed to have grown stronger some months later when already the government was flirting with the idea that the project might cost $10 billion.

The scheme also began to be interpreted by the nationalist Left as part of the energy and resources sellout to the United States. There was little doubt, especially after the Nixon surcharge measures on August 15, 1971, that the United States government increasingly was thinking of Canada as a safe supplier of the raw materials needed to feed the U.S. military-industrial machine, and as not much else. The United States already had control of most of Canada's resource extraction industries, and there was increasing pressure for the exportation of Canadian energy to the States. This energy would feed an industrial machine, enable it to operate more efficiently, and thereby lessen Canada's own chances of diversifying her economy by creating industries capable of competing on continental and international markets. The Canadian nationalist argument was summed up by the headline of an article written by James Laxer, a leader of the left-wing group then within the socialist New Democratic Party: "Give us your oil, give us your power, give us your water — but don't give us your cars."

Many questions were asked — and they remain unanswered — about the price at which the surplus energy from the James Bay project would be sold to the United States. Would this electricity be sold at production cost, expected to be twice that of other Quebec-produced power? Or would its higher production cost be absorbed within Quebec by raising local tariffs? If that happened, and the electricity was then sold to the States at that price, the Quebec people in effect would be subsidizing electricity consumers in New York.

The "continental energy deal" has become a poker

game in which access for Canadian oil to the U.S. market (oil that is already American owned, in any case) is traded off against Canada's willingness to export natural gas, electricity and water. Canadian governments seemed anxious to sell, in accordance with a long-held precept that the country needs American money. But Kierans was arguing that Canada should play it cool, hold back, refuse to sell, because in twenty years the world would be in even more desperate need of raw material and energy. Canada cannot lose by waiting. And the waiting would provide lead time in which the nation could really examine its reserves and decide what it wants to do with them. [5]

Despite Bourassa's highly publicized meetings with the Rockefellers, Rothschilds, Rio Tinto and other foreign businessmen, the James Bay Corporation at an early stage began to soft-pedal the possibility of American involvement. The argument then became that the project was needed to fill an energy gap to be felt in Quebec in 1978. Quebec is doubling its power demand every eight or ten years. Even with the big developments at Manic and Churchill Falls coming into the system (Churchill in 1972 and on an ascending scale until 1976, Manic 5 already absorbed into the system, and Manic 3 in 1975-76), a gap would again begin to open up late in the decade. So far, no one has been able to challenge these projections; apparently no one in Quebec other than Hydro-Quebec has the necessary information. However, many people felt uneasy that such a huge project was being justified on the advice of an agency with a built-in vested interest in its own growth — and which is engaged in a ceaseless advertising campaign to persuade people to consume more electricity. These expert predictions, it must be noted, seem to be fairly flexible, for Bourassa began to backtrack slightly as his scheme came under criticism in Ottawa and Toronto. Hydro-Quebec, he said nearly a year later, was now advising him that the power would not be needed before 1979 or 1980. Anyway, how did this demand, which, if accurately forecast, would absorb all of the James Bay power, fit into the plans to sell the power to the United States? The arguments became more incoherent as time passed. It became difficult to disagree with the summary made by a group of Montreal social scicnce researchers called the Friends of the North Committee. "The overriding use of the James Bay project is not to furnish electric power at any rate," they wrote. "It is only an excuse for a giant boondoggle that gives big finance and big business the opportunity to get their hands into the public till."

Supposing the power *is* needed by 1978, is the James Bay project the most economical, the most fruitful way of producing it from the point of view of the province's economic development? None of these questions had been answered a whole year after Bourassa's announcement. Studies, of course, were underway, but they had built into them the characteristic of self-fulfilling prophecy. Like the earlier engineering reports, these studies could be trusted to come to the right conclusions. At one point the possible justifications for the scheme became so wild that a spokesman for the James Bay Development Corporation said the company officials would be the happiest people in Canada if it proved possible to use all the power in the area itself, without exporting it to other parts of Quebec. [6] This was a fantastic statement because the amounts of power being considered would double the present generating capacity of the province, while the largest population projected for the area is only 100,000 people. It was an indication of the strange air of unreality that still hangs around this project.

Would the power produced be economic in the markets in which it would have to be sold? Immediately after Bourassa's announcement the claim was made that it would be, by 1978.[7] But nearly a year later it was admitted that detailed cost studies were still underway.[8] It was known that the electricity produced from Churchill Falls in Labrador (and bought by Hydro-Quebec under a long-term contract) would cost 4.89 mills until 1981, and be reduced by stages to 3.98 mills after the year 2000. The best estimates about James Bay were that the first power would cost 9 or 10 mills.[9] (By May 1972, the officially estimated cost of James Bay power was 11.8 mills.) It was argued, however, that by the time the power was available for sale, other power sources would be producing electricity at similar costs. Lionel Cahill of Hydro-Quebec argued vigorously before the Hydro-Quebec commissioners that hydro power would continue to be competitive. Though construction costs for thermal stations were about half of those for hydroelectric stations, he said, operating costs were continuing to climb. Thermal station electricity which used to cost an average of $125 per kilowatt-hour would cost $325 by 1980, and the life expectancy of thermal stations was only 35 years compared with 50 years for a hydroelectric station. Whereas hydro stations required no fuel, the cost of oil for thermal stations had risen from $2.30 a barrel in 1969 to $3.85 in 1971. A hydro station could reach 80 percent utilization, but the trustworthiness of thermal stations exceeding 500,000 kilowatts was doubtful. The cost of nuclear stations in the United States, now averaging about $225 per kilowatt-hour, would be up to $350 a kilowatt-hour in 1980. Cahill summed up his argument by saying that the NBR complex would provide power at lower prices than from any other possible source.

Strangely, Cahill did not supply comparable figures per kilowatt-hour for the James Bay project. Indeed, of the three preliminary reports, only one mentioned a cost per installed kilowatt — $575, about double Cahill's figures for the other forms of energy. No facts were produced supporting Cahill's statement that James Bay energy would be cheaper. He did not say so in his summary, later published, but the power from Churchill Falls cost $181,818 per megawatt installed at the point of origin. The Pickering nuclear station which was put into the Ontario system early in 1972 cost $335,849 per megawatt installed. On the basis of Bourassa's expected expenditure, the James Bay cost would be $738,314 per megawatt installed. In other words, it would be *two and a half* times more expensive than the nuclear power at Pickering. Hydro power has certain advantages when the cost is worked out by kilowatt-hours produced, yet even using this method, no advantages seemed to lie with the James Bay project. Pickering power was costing between 5 and 6 mills, compared with the 4.81 mills that had been expected. A comparable coal-burning plant at Nanticoke in Ontario was costing 5.28 mills and James Bay, so far as anyone could tell, would cost 9 or 10 mills delivered in Montreal. [10]

These suspicions were reinforced in February, 1972, when someone in Hydro-Quebec leaked the information [11] that a study done by the American firm, United Engineers and Constructors Ltd. of Philadelphia, said that Hydro-Quebec could, between 1978 and 1980, build nuclear generators with a total effective capacity of 5,500 megawatts which would produce electricity at costs between 7.1 mills and 9.9 mills per kilowatt-hour.

Thermal plants would cost between 9 and 11.4 mills, and the James Bay power, on the basis of the original consultants' studies, would cost 10 mills delivered in Montreal.

Around the same time this information was made public, Bourassa was asked about speculation that the total cost of the James Bay project might reach $10 billion. He refused to deny it. He said it was still too early to say. It depended, he said, on how much of the proposed project would be built, on whether the interest rate would be 8.5 percent or 10 percent, on whether inflation was allowed for at 4 percent or 5 percent. That sort of data was still being studied.

The figures used by Hydro-Quebec to justify their scheme when they announced in May, 1972, that construction would start on the La Grande River were not much more informative than these earlier estimates. They claimed—voluminously, for the premier of the province claimed he had 25 expert studies which now supported his decision to proceed with the James Bay project — that the power at 11.8 mills per kilowatt hour would be cheaper than nuclear power that would be available at the same time, in the early 1980's. But again Jacques Parizeau drove a coach and horses through the argument: the comparisons were made with small and expensive nuclear stations, he argued, not with the large and more cheaply run stations that would be working both in France and the United States when James Bay power comes on power. It was like, he said, comparing a new car with the horse and buggy.

No one answered this charge.

As part of the fantastic atmosphere which had grown to surround the whole project, the corporation was talking about the possibility of processing all the minerals to be exploited, right there in the area itself, although apparently no studies had been done to indicate whether it made any economic sense to process them there instead of sending them directly to Pittsburgh or Montreal. When pressed, officials of the corporation would admit that it was possible that local processing of minerals might be found uneconomic, in which case it would not be done. Would not this mean then, that the minerals would be sold off directly to the Americans, as so many other Canadian riches had been? Well, they would reply, it could perhaps happen, in theory.

The question of mineral rights and forest rights in the area has been little discussed in public, but some people believe it might hold the key to the whole rationale for the project. It has been a pattern of northern and mid-northern development in Canada to spend great sums of public money on road and rail access to mineral resources which have then been exploited at high profit by private companies. The James Bay area has been one of the areas least affected by these pushes into the north. At the end of 1971, it was argued by one commentator[12] that Bourassa was really seeking an excuse to allow the building of a communications infrastructure to open up that area to the mining companies. André Charbonneau recalled that in 1957 Great Whale Iron Mines Ltd. hoped to exploit 400 million tons of iron concentrate from a mine on the Great Whale River, but the scheme had foundered on the proposed $300 million cost of a port to service the mine. A hundred miles farther south, Duncan Range Iron Mines Ltd. hoped to extract 5 million tons of iron ore annually for forty years, and was ready to invest $150 million. The road from the south fortuitously passes within five miles of the iron ore; and in 1972 the company president wrote enthusiastic letters to newspapers praising the project. Many other companies have spent a lot of money exploring for minerals in the project area. Among them are Nemiscau Mines, a subsidiary of International Nickel, which has rights in the area of Lac Chabouillette, supposedly rich in copper; Chessbar Iron Powder Company, which claims reserves of 40 million tons of iron near Lake Theodat; Coniagas Company, said to have discovered copper; and Quebec Sturgeon Mines and Falconbridge Nickel, which have undertaken prospecting work. Mineral development has been held up by the inaccessibility of the region and lack of electricity. Now, the James Bay project promises to overcome both difficulties because 500 miles of project roads can be used for access to the mines, and the mines can take advantage of the electricity to be brought from the Abitibi and Lake St. Jean regions to power construction on the new dams. Could this be the main motive for the project? Charbonneau's argument is supported by the corporation's having pressed on immediately with only one thing: road building.

By early 1972 opinion among people in Montreal who had taken an interest in the project was divided. One group thought it could never happen, it was a non-event, an impossibility, the money could not be found, it was a sellout on a scale intolerable to any federal government, and Bourassa would eventually have to abandon his pet scheme.

Another group, however, believed that the power was needed so desperately by Americans that they would stop at nothing to get it. The news that negotiations for selling the power to the New York State Power Grid were already well advanced seemed to support this view. This group also thought that what was really at stake, aside from the question of U.S. power needs, was vast mineral riches. The Sierra Club of Ontario at this time filed an intervention in any application that might come before the National Energy Board for the exportation of Canadian electrical power to the United States.

Bourassa himself was still talking about the project as "one of the most audacious enterprises of the century." Yet a hint of the public's general bewilderment was given in 1972 at Bourassa's annual meeting with the Employers' Council of Quebec, when the council furnished its usual memoire about the budgetary priorities of his government. Bourassa told the gathering he was astonished to see no mention of the James Bay project in the list.

"We will include it," replied the president of the council, "when we know what it is."

Notes For Chapter VII:
1: May 5, 1971.
2: Le Devoir, May 13 and 14, 1971.
3: For an account of this see Gordon to Watkins to You, A Documentary on the Battle for Control of our Economy, published by New Press, Toronto.
4: Same as 2.
5: Kierans resigned April 29 (the same day as Bourassa's announcement). His argument is developed in full in his speech to the Canadian Economics Association annual meeting, St. John's, Newfoundland, June 3, 1971.
6: André Langlois, James Bay Corporation coordinator, speaking at a meeting in November, 1971, called by the Société pour Vaincre la Pollution.
7: Dominique Clift, Montreal Star, May 11, 1971.
8: R. G. Gibbens, business editor, Montreal Star, March 2, 1971.
9: Articles by Gibbens on April 27 and Clift on May 11, Montreal Star; André Chenier, La Presse, May 11, 1971.
10: André Chenier, La Presse, May 11.
11: Québec-Presse, February 6, 1972, and Financial Post, Toronto, February 12.
12: André Charbonneau, article Les Maîtres de la Radissonie, in the special issue La Baie James des Amérindiennes, of the Recherches Amérindiennes au Quebec, December, 1971.

8. What The Indian Can Teach

The hunting camps in which the Indians live most of the winter are deep in the bush, 50 to 150 miles from the settlements. Nowadays it is customary for the families to fly to the camps. But in former days they travelled by canoe, using as highways the great rivers which are now to be dammed and controlled. "I remember the days," says Hilda Diamond, mother of Chief Billy Diamond of Rupert House, "when I used to carry two children on my back over portages five and six miles long, as we went up the Nottaway by canoe to our hunting camps. We used to leave in September and never come back until the end of May. As soon as the rivers are diverted, those portages and trips will no longer be available. Those rivers were the highways for the Indians. I still have memories of how I used to live, and I would like my grandchildren to live like that, too."

Mrs. Diamond is one of a breed rare nowadays outside these Indian communities — a superb cook, the center of a great family of children, grandchildren and relations, the sort of woman who adopts small ones when her own family is grown. The little house in which she lives in Rupert House was jammed with people when we arrived there in February during a tour of the region. Her daughter Annie had just returned from the trap line with her family. Her husband was there and her sons with their wives and children. For someone like myself from the typical nuclear family of the city, the crowded house — hardly ever fewer than fifteen, sometimes as many as twenty-five people, of all ages — seemed incredibly warm and vital.

I talked to dozens of Indians of all ages and of differing backgrounds — old men retired from hunting, active middle-aged hunters, middle-aged men who have gone into the wage economy, youngsters who have gone back to hunting, and youngsters who hardly know one end of a moose from the other. Yet they were impressively united in the face of the James Bay project. They were all against it.

The first reason they gave was that the project would damage the animals, and therefore damage the Indians. These communities still have at the center of their attitudes a deep respect for nature, for the animals, and a firm belief that a meaningful life depends on maintaining the balance. This belief lingers even in the younger people who no longer hunt or trap, and do not even know how to do it. Still very much part of their emotional background is their perceptive need for the land — their knowledge, in the words of one study,[1] that "an Indian can go on to the land whenever he wishes, and by exercising acumen and inherent ability, gain a livelihood in the tradition of his forefathers."

This perception is strong even in Fort George, to the north of the James Bay project area, a place run by a strong white establishment of 200 people, where most of the work is performed for a network of governmental institutions such as schools and a hospital. Perhaps only 5 percent of the Indian families living there still trap for a living, but many of those who have given it up and gone into the wage economy return to the bush regularly to kill bush food. Some 40 percent of these families still depend on country food that they kill themselves (their dependence is on the order of 70 percent). Some are young men who did not go to school until they were well into their late teens or early twenties, and spent their early lives on the trap lines with their fathers. They are the kind of Indians who might be supposed by the white man to have a vested interest in developments such as the James Bay project, for will such development not bring work into their area?

The fact is that such young men appear to be 100 percent against the project, not only because they are still devoted to nature, to the wilderness and to the animals, but also because they know what experience has proven: that Indians never prosper from big developmental projects forced on them from the south. At most they will get some jobs — usually of a menial kind — for a few years. But then what? Why, then it will be too late. The rivers will be dammed and nature will be destroyed. The white men, with their insensitivity toward animals, will be slaughtering and leaving carcasses lying about to rot. Electricity will be pouring south, worked by dials and buttons. And as the Cree leaders say, the Indians will be out of work, on welfare; their women used by the white transients; their best workers degenerated by liquor, bewilderment and alienation.

The most startling fact revealed to me during this trip was that the Indians have an utterly clear knowledge of what will happen to them when the James Bay project arrives, and do not need to be instructed in what is best

Smally Petawabano, Chief of the Mistassini Cree band for the past 15 years.

Chief Robert Kanatewat of the Fort George band.

Mistassini trapper William Matoush: "The whites are coming to flood the forest. They teach the Indians how to build dams to drown the land. Ourselves, we can teach them how to look at nature. We grew up with it. We were born with it. Our job is to protect it, not destroy it. Nature is our mother."

Annie Neeposh, a magnificent 85-year-old Cree woman, photographed in the family hunting camp: "There is only one thing good in all of it: we won't have to go far for our water."

for them by any number of button-pushing, southern decision makers. In Mistassini, where the hunting life is still firmly entrenched, this knowledge is held even more strongly. The invariable answer to any question about the James Bay project was, "We are thinking about the animals." The land is to be flooded; the land is to be destroyed. If they destroy the land, they destroy the animals, and they destroy the Indian. "When we don't kill so many beaver as we could," said William Matoush, an old hunter in Mistassini, "it is like putting something away in the bank. The beaver are our savings. Now if the white man is going to come and flood the land he is wiping out our savings. We talk about it among ourselves. We cannot stop it. We are getting old. But we have to think of our grandchildren, and look to them to see what they can do about it."

"The white men can learn a lot from Indians, mainly about nature," Matoush told me. "White men are going to come and flood the land. That's teaching the Indians how to flood land and build dams. But when it comes to nature we can tell them what to think about nature. We were raised with nature. We were born with it. We have got to look after it. Not to destroy it. It's like the mother, for us."

Out in a hunting camp, Annie Neeposh, more than eighty-five years old, and a tremendously alert, powerful, matriarchal figure, sat on the spruce-bough floor which gave a delicious scent to the family tent and said: "The only good thing about the project is that we won't have so far to go for water."

The hunting camps are astonishing, for everything in them is handmade. Although the hunting families are submerged in the Canadian winter, to them it is not a harsh environment but the very life that sustains them. The hunter splits the logs and chooses the boughs from which he will make his house. The walls are tightly packed and insulated with moss; boughs are bent over to support the canvas roof. The stove is made from an old can; the chimney is shaped from a piece of tin. The wood for the fire is gathered, sawed, and stacked before the door in piles designed to break the winter winds. A network of stripped logs is strung under the roof, somewhat like rafters, from which all sorts of things are hung during the long winter. Pliable tamarack boughs are bent into circular frames on which the beaver skins are stretched and dried. The snowshoes which are still the hunter's only means of transportation in the bush during the winter are laboriously bent into shape and strung with moose hide. The result is remarkably beautiful — the James Bay Cree snowshoe. It has never found its way into the shops of the south because it is made only when needed. The sled the hunter pulls behind him also is handmade — many still make the runners from a mixture of ice and mud — and so is the snow shovel. Some of the clothing, especially the moccasins, is made from moose hides, prepared by the women according to a traditional and laborious process which involves many scrapings, soakings, dryings, and finally a smoking over a fire that comes from a particular type of standing dead wood, the gathering of which is itself a major operation. On top of all that, the hunter raises his children in the arts of their ancestors — the arts of survival, the only ones which had any significance for them in their traditional lives — and catches most of his own food. Around all the camps hang bones of various kinds, the means by which the hunters show their respect for the animals. At one of the camps I visited, bear bones had been carefully wrapped in bark and tied around the trunk of two trees. No one messes around with bear bones. Beaver bones, particularly the head, arms and tail, are preserved, placed in a bag and put up in the bone tree. The rest of the bones are returned to the water from which the beaver came. Strings of rabbit skulls still adorn almost every Indian hunter's home.

"If we allow a dog to get hold of the bones," said William Matoush, "we will have a hard time killing that animal. He will become scarce."

In Rupert House, John Blackned, a seventy-eight-year-old hunter, said that everyone in the community, including the young, has respect for the birds. All his life has been adjusted to the great geese migrations, which last about three weeks in spring and autumn. It is important that everything be used, and the traditional rituals be respected. When the goose is killed, a special cake has to be made and eaten first. All of the first kill has to be eaten and shared, whether it is one goose or ten. Before the first meat is tasted, a piece must be put in the fire. None of the goose bones are thrown away; all are put up in a tree in a bag. The head is stuffed and ornamental beadwork made on it. "The Indian does not like the disrespect that white men show for the geese," said Blackned. "For all these years Indians have respected the geese, and now we find white men do not eat the parts that should be respected — they just eat what they want and throw the rest away. I have seen years when there are many young, and other years when there are few young birds. But now we have more white hunters here, and some of these white men seem to think the geese will always continue to grow, so they kill too many."

Another old trapper in Fort George, George Pachana, whose trap line lies on the La Grande River and will be entirely submerged by flooding, said: "I am not interested in it at all. I am not interested in the money.

Even if this project is all closed down, we will survive. We do not need it. At any time I would be glad to hear that this thing is stopped."

Robert Kanatewat, a health worker and chief of the Fort George band, said: "They are already building roads. There goes your nature right away. Our people want to go back to the land whenever they feel like it. They will never go down south to the labor market. They will always be here in this last remote area that has never been trod by any white man, and when this is gone, there is nothing left. It is just like destroying these people completely."

Sam Tapiatic went through a grade-12 education in the white man's system, and has lived many years in the south, in Ottawa and other cities. He told me in Fort George, "People here cannot live like the white man, working every day. They like to think they can go back to the land any time they feel like it. It would be all right if they could find a means to get electricity without destroying the land. What would happen if this whole area was filled with cities? Where would *we* go then?" His brother Eddie, twenty-six, supervisor of boys at the school hostel in Fort George said: "Most of the people do not want money to live. They want to go out and live the way they do, hunting. Personally I like the way it is here right now. I was south when I was younger, and I got sick and tired of cities."

The two sides of the James Bay confrontation are quite clearly defined, and so are their aims. On the one side, the white men want money, power and wealth, and they think the Indians should want some of these too. But the white men have a problem. For the Indians, quite genuinely, do not seem to be interested in money, and they seem to reject every scheme dreamed up by the white man for the well-being of the Indians. The things that mean most to the Indians — the animals, nature, wild rivers, clean air and water — are the very things that the white man is preparing to sell for money. The Indian struggle now is to stop him from doing it.

A few Indians have been employed on early work on the project, cutting bush to make roads. Some Indians I talked with felt that Indians should not help the white man to destroy the land in this way. But to the Indians these were just the sort of jobs that crop up from time to time, and no one would really condemn a family man for taking the work. It is, nevertheless, essentially casual work: the men working in the wilderness northwest of Mistassini were on contract from January 6 to February 25 and were guaranteed $800 a man, minus expenses. Unfortunately, the terms of this contract are not at all like those under which white laborers are usually employed in the Canadian north — their travelling expenses, lodging and food are almost invariably paid, as well as a special northern allowance. The Indians have to pay for all their own food, and fly it into the bush camp at their own expense. They have to get themselves into and out of the bush, the only way being by plane, and they have to depend on their Indian band manager to see to it they do not run out of food. (The band supplies this service for the construction company, but is paid nothing for it.) In all, the chief at Mistassini, Smally Petawabano, estimated that when the expenses are paid, the men are lucky to clear $40 a week.

I have no doubt at all that the Indians do not want the changes being forced on them by the James Bay project. They have proven remarkably adaptable and resilient, but only within a context in which they could absorb change into the fabric of their cultural beliefs and their life styles. The James Bay project is on a different scale. The Indian life, as an Indian life, is going to be destroyed, and the white man looks forward — at his most generous — to attaching the Indians in some way to the labor force in the area.

"Our bands have officially expressed opposition to the project," wrote the Mistassini and Waswanipi bands to Indian Affairs Minister Jean Chrétien, in March, 1972. "We are exploring every means of protecting our way of life which is being threatened. We have had independent legal advice that you as minister, your department, and the federal government, have powers which could be used to protect our interests. We have been told these powers can be used to protect our way of life, our animals, and our lands on which we depend. Our desire is that you should exercise some of these powers." The Indians then asked the minister to report to them exactly what powers he had for protecting their way of life, when, where and how successfully he had ever exercised such powers in other parts of Canada in similar circumstances, and what they could do to get him to take some action on their behalf. They asked for an early reply because construction had already started in the region.

Some researchers in Montreal have suggested that the government has a case to answer under the International Convention on the Crime of Genocide. This convention defines genocide as "denial of the right of existence of entire human groups," and the crime as any of a number of acts committed with intent to destroy, in whole or in part, a national, ethnical, racial or religious group. Two of these acts, "causing serious bodily or mental harm to members of the group, and deliberately inflicting on the group conditions of life calculated to bring about its physical destruction in whole or in part," would appear to have some relevance to the James Bay situation. Canada ratified the convention, but excused itself from passing enabling legislation. Other people argue that although there is no law under which the Quebec premier could be charged with genocide, a campaign mounted along these lines could prove terribly embarrassing, and an effective form of political pressure.

If that doesn't work and if in fact nothing else works, the Indians will have to fall back on *medew* (pronounced "med-e-o"), the special power of a hunter, still possessed by a number of shamans among these hunting bands, to perform magic and witchcraft. Belief in this power is strong, even among the young Indians. I have been told in confidence by several young people that one of these days a shaman will put a curse on the James Bay project, and stop it.

If it comes to that, it will be a battle between two witchcrafts, theirs and ours. The James Bay project could have been dreamed up only by a society with a fanatical belief in the supernatural authority of its own witchcraft — technological progress.

Note For Chapter VIII:
1: *Canada North. Man and the Land,* by John K. Naysmith, of Northern Economic Development Branch, Ottawa.

Epilog or
The Destruction
Begins

By the fall of 1972 scores of millions of dollars worth of work had been done on the James Bay project, but a strange silence still surrounded the issue. The government's efforts to justify the project had been unconvincing, but had still not been subjected to any rigorous analysis.

It appeared that the government had pulled off a coup by deciding to go ahead first with the La Grande section of the project, that part which lies farthest north from Montreal, for the farther north the government went, the more remote the project became in the public mind.

The government had succeeded in convincing the people of the province that there "is nothing there." In that remote place, the argument runs, the trees are sparse and small, and of no commercial value. The Indians have largely given up trapping, and have moved into the wage economy. From the environmental and social points of view, the northern project was preferable, argued the government, with an air of sanctity.

"The James Bay Development Corporation is determined to develop without destroying," said the corporation when it released its report on the Initial Phase
of the project. "Its action must consolidate the
ecological balance, not upset it." Further on, the corporation wrote: "The development of James Bay opens a
fascinating vista for the James Bay Indians. It provides
them with a choice: to continue to live off the land hunting and fishing and/or to become part of a new lifestyle
which some of them already have experienced in Montreal or in other southern communities."

With this kind of vague rhetoric the corporation
managed to convey the impression that it was concerned
about the Indians and the environment.

This impression was reflected in the sort of editorial
that appeared in *The Montreal Star* a day or two after
the corporation released its report: "The data released
with the announcement indicates that both social and
ecological considerations played a major part in the
decision . . . the complex is sufficiently far north that the
work to be undertaken . . . is likely to result in minimum
disruption to both people and resources in the region."

The assumption that because something is happening
farther north, therefore disruption will be less, is almost
the exact opposite of the facts, and it would be interesting to know just what the assumption is based on.
Indeed, the claim that there is really "nothing there" is
one of the most successful uses of the "Big Lie" since
Goebbels. In many respects, to proceed with the northern project first is *worse* than if the government had
gone ahead in the south first. Being farther north, indeed
just below the treeline, the northern project will be in
country where the flora and fauna is at its northern limit,
and is therefore in a more fragile balance than farther
south. Interventions in this borderline area could

have even more drastic results than they might have in an area of more abundant plant life.

The other assumption, that ecological considerations have influenced the choice of area to be flooded first, seems to suggest that the authorities had done some ecological work before making their choice. That is quite untrue, and it is incredibly lazy of the newspapers and other media not to have discovered that there are no facts to back up these bold claims for environmental virtue.

More startling, perhaps, is the utter silence of the media on the government's double-faced performance about the Caniapiscau (see chapter five). The government's ecological task force recommended against blocking off this river: after all, it runs directly north, through tundra, and interference with its course would very seriously extend the range of possible effects into a different and more difficult type of country. Nevertheless, the announced scheme depends heavily on the creation of a vast reservoir at the headwaters of the Caniapiscau. No one has asked the government, the corporation, or Hydro-Quebec to explain their violation of their own decision to respect the recommendations of their own task force.

It is not surprising, perhaps, that the public is more or less apathetic about what is happening in James Bay: it has other things to worry about (though one would think that even the public might be likely to scrutinize carefully the spending of $5.8 billion of public money). I must admit that it was not until I went myself along the La Grande River in August of 1972 that I realized the enormity of the scheme and the utter folly of the proposed destruction of a wilderness that must be one of the most superb on the continent. In that month the Indians of Quebec Association mobilized a task force of scientists to make a report on the environmental consequences of the scheme for the Indian life in the area. They financed this investigation from a $250,000 grant given them by the federal government — and it is highly significant, in view of some of the arguments I have made earlier in this book in the sections dealing with Indians, that their first action reflected the Indian concern for nature and the land.

I went up the river three times with groups of Indians, the young accompanying the old. Even the younger Indians who no longer live in the bush as full-time trappers, go into the bush, or out onto the bay, almost every weekend, in search of wild food around which their entire culture is built. At one season they hunt ducks and geese. At another time they are after caribou. They hunt rabbits and porcupine, and when the fish are running they catch them in netsful and tubsful, and share them around. When they shoot a bear, the village has plenty of meat. The anthropologists who went with the task force discovered that every Indian family in Fort George gets about half its food from the bush.

The scientists with the task force, under the leadership of Dr. John Spence of McGill University, established quite clearly that there is no way that the Indian life in the bush can co-exist with a scheme on the vast scale of the one that now stands on the drawing boards. The Indian life in the bush will be drowned. Such an action can be contemplated only on the assumption that these people, this culture, their way of life, is meaningless.

We went one weekend to the first rapids on the La Grande, an astonishingly beautiful place where for generations people have pulled their canoes onto the rocky shore and camped for a few days while the whitefish are running up the river to their spawning beds beneath the rapids. (The scientists at first insisted that the whitefish must be shooting the rapids and spawning farther inland; but the Indians finally convinced them that this wasn't the case.) The La Grande River is one of the most superb in Canada, almost a mile wide in its lower reaches, but narrowing to a few hundred yards (still big by southern standards!) where the water boils furiously over the rapids. Just there the rocks on the shore are broad, striated, multi-colored slabs. As the men clamber around the rocks with their nets, timing their throw with the surging and falling of the white water, one is keenly aware of living in harmony with the power of nature. And one senses from these people the great joy they have in it, the inner peace it brings them. Even the young ones seem emotionally tied to the land, the river and the continuous changes around the shores.

We walked away from the rapids through the bush, springing up and down as much as a foot on the soggy muskeg, to higher ground where the deciduous trees are scattered and the ground is covered with soft green lichen. Under this is a layer of moisture, almost as if the entire country is covered with water, as if the rivers and multitudinous lakes are only the visible part of a remarkably complex drainage system. There we snapped short boughs off young spruce trees for use as the floor of our tent. The place was so quiet, peaceful, a corner of paradise hidden away on this turbulent continent.

Right there, the white men from the south are going to make a huge gravel pit, right there where for generations these people have enjoyed their land and the life that grows on it. Right where the rapids are, where the whitefish spawn, the white men from the south will build a power house, to be known, in the engineer's jargon, as LG 1.

To the engineers, these glorious rapids are, in the

words used in the Initial Phase Plan — "a vast potential now wasting in foam and swirls." They will replace them with "a powerhouse and spillway that form an integral part of the dam, which will consist of zoned embankments constructed of clay, sand and gravel, and rockfill. The powerhouse will be located in the river channel and will contain eight units each with 115,000 kilowatts capacity — an installed capacity of 920,000 kilowatts."

The whitefish at these rapids provide the Indians of Fort George with 12 percent of their diet. These fish will, the scientists under Dr. Spence concluded, be completely eliminated by the dam.

Later, in two canoes full of young and older Indians, we ran right up through swirling waters to these rapids and portaged the two or three hundred yards over them. It is only fifteen years since the older trappers have had motors on their canoes. Before that they paddled up the river every fall, carried their canoes, their supplies and their families over as many as thirty portages, on some of which they would have to walk for an hour, and they would be on the river for fourteen days before they reached their trapping grounds.

The Indians still build the traditional teepees on the river banks, still set their nets and their snares in the waters and the forest of the river valley, still feed themselves handsomely through their skill and their profound knowledge of the land and the animals with which man shares the earth. "I have heard many people call this land our garden," said Job Bearskin, a fifty-nine-year-old trapper with whom we travelled. "In this garden things grow and multiply. The Indians are one of the things which grow there. We all love our garden."

The concept of man as an integral part of nature — a truth that is just being rediscovered by worried white men — could not be more explicitly, simply and beautifully expressed than by Mr. Bearskin, who is without doubt one of the most remarkable men I have ever had the honor to meet. We went with him about seventy miles up the river to the place the Indians call Squirrel Rapids — another lovely spot, but now known and even celebrated in Montreal as LG 2. At this place the white men will build a dam rising 450 feet above the river. Behind that dam, the land will be flooded for 70 miles upstream, and the huge lake will increase the water surface of that land from 80 square miles — the river beds and small lakes — to 1,550 square miles. Until one flies over this huge country and tries to visualize the lake as it will be, it is difficult to conceive its magnitude. And when one grasps that, it is hard to believe that there are men who think our country will be improved by the creation of such vast bodies of water in this complex and interesting place.

Mr. Bearskin comes from a culture which values the beauty of this place, and places a value on everything growing in a land that to the uninstructed eye is just a vast emptiness. His people, for instance, protect the food on which the animals live, guard carefully the trees that the rabbit and porcupine like to eat, rejoice when they see the signs of the bear at the rocks under which the succulent ants are to be found. Occasionally, he says, men may use a tree for something; but not often. They never cut trees down unnecessarily. I went with him to the construction camp hacked by the white man out of the bush on a hill overlooking the Squirrel Rapids. The whole concept, the whole approach, was an offence to Mr. Bearskin.

The camp was a flat, dusty sandpile, surrounded by a tangled mass of uprooted trees. "All along the river," he reported back to a meeting of trappers in Fort George,

"I have seen signs of the white man's destruction. They have destroyed much already. They have brought up the earth from underneath. Those places you have always loved to look at, they are no longer so beautiful. His work is only starting. What will it be like when he is finished?"

"The installed capacity," says the Initial Phase Plan about LG 2 "will be 4,410,000 kilowatts. This underground installation will be the most important of the entire complex, and will constitute the first stage of development." I sat with the trapper on a rock beside the Squirrel Rapids, and told him that where we sat there would be no river, that the rapids would be no more, because the water is to be blocked upstream by the dam, taken around the back of a hill, and dropped through a powerhouse 500 feet underground, before being fed back into the river below where we sat. He could not believe it. He was shocked. "It will not be natural," he said.

Two miles downstream, just where a glorious little stream tumbles over rocks into the La Grande, an aircraft landing base has been built. Though this would be one of the most beautiful spots for tourism, if in future tourism is to be encouraged (as the James Bay Corporation says it is), an area of two hundred-year-old trees has been wiped clean right beside these beautiful rapids. Just here, Mr. Bearskin used to pick up his canoe on his shoulders and begin the long trek overland through a system of lakes as he wended his way slowly to his trap line. He could hardly believe what the white man had done to his portaging place.

And so it goes on. The work has hardly started. So far it consists mostly of road and camp construction. We went farther inland to the abandoned Kanaaupscow post of the Hudson's Bay Company, where the Indians used to sit around a huge theater rock watching for their friends to come down the Kanaaupscow River in the spring after their winter in the bush. The rock is full of legends and associations; at the burial ground on the slope of a nearby hill seventeen graves are placed to face the rising sun. The country is full of animals. Mr. Bearskin traps right across the river from where we sat. He has never missed a winter in the bush in his life. The whole river valley is covered by the trap lines of Indian hunters from Fort George, Great Whale River, and even from Mistassini, far inland. These lands will be flooded; the Indians are expected just to move over.

Destruction of nature on a really colossal scale is being undertaken in the James Bay area, and still neither the provincial nor the federal government has commissioned any serious environmental studies. Dr. Spence's task force, which had only three weeks in which to examine the resources on which the Indians live, produced the first study that carried any scientific authority at all. They found, for example, that already oil pollution in the rivers is severe, and fish are dying (something confirmed by all of the trappers). The sturgeon, an important fish to the Indians, which spawns inland at Sakami Rapids and Lake, can be expected to disappear completely, and, judging by Russian experience, never to reappear.

In the land behind LG 2, the beaver, now clinging to the shorelines of lakes and rivers, will have no chance of re-establishing themselves on what will be the rocky shorelines of the immense new lake. Still farther up the La Grande there will eventually be two more dams, and according to one plan which has never been officially announced, at the headwaters of the Caniapiscau one of the three or four highest dams in the world will be built, creating a lake of maybe 3,000 square miles — certainly one of the biggest man-made lakes on earth. This would inundate an important valley for caribou migration, eliminate the rapids which the caribou use to escape pursuing wolf packs, and cover with 70 to 80 feet of water all the spawning beds of the ouananish, the land-locked salmon which now attract many American fishermen to a number of fishing camps. The scientists were able to establish, even in their rushed observations, that the potential for developing renewable resources along the La Grande River will be entirely destroyed by the scheme as now planned. The speckled trout, which spawn in the bottom of the rapids, and depend on the fast-flowing water bringing down lots of food, will be wiped out, for all the rapids along this magnificent river will be eliminated as the dammed water rises and creeps across the land.

The scientists established that large areas of the new lakes will be extremely shallow: the shorelines will be dotted with dead trees standing out of the water, which inevitably means that the surface of the lakes will be covered with floating logs. Draw-downs will be 20 to 30 feet annually at LG 2, and as much as 50 feet at Caniapiscau. Geese flight patterns have already been affected, and it is clear that some of the most important islands for shooting geese, just off the mouth of the La Grande River, will be damaged by increased erosion. Hydrologists working with the Indians' task force believe that from the engineers' own figures, it seems likely that river flows will almost cease for a year while the work is underway: this would dry up the Fort George water supply. Mind you, there is already severe water pollution in Fort George, which can only increase with an influx of more white men into the town. The result will be an increase in diseases such as dysentery among children. (Half of the scientists themselves got diarrhea when they drank the water.) No plans to deal with these problems have been made.

It can be seen then that an environmental disaster of a

spectacular kind is in the making in James Bay: that half of the food supply of the Indian people of that area will be eliminated (making them more dependent on the store food that already depresses the quality of their lives); that trappers who have always occupied and never surrendered this land are to be simply dispossessed; and that huge sums of public money are being wasted in pursuit of these ignoble aims.

What is happening in James Bay is a public scandal, but no newspaper wishes to reveal it. The waste of public money is utterly incredible. Dozens of helicopters are flying around at costs of between $250 and $650 an hour. Everything is moved by helicopter; it cost some $5,000 to move a caterpiller earth-moving machine a half hour flight from one site to the next. Gasoline is flown in, and then shuttled around by helicopter, a barrel at a time. Even the people working on the site and the scheme seem sceptical as to its viability. The money is pouring down the drain every minute of the day. (Construction chiefs who did not know who we were confessed to us their apprehension that twice as much money was being spent as need be; and said that the James Bay Corporation could save $30,000,000 by building a dock at Moosonee and bringing material in by barge, but will not do it because Moosonee is in Ontario.)

One has only to keep one's ears open to know that already racist sentiments of the most crude kind are being expressed by transient white men about Indians. The process of Indian degeneration has already gone a stage further than a year ago: Indian women are already being used ("for the price of a drink," as the visitors will tell you contemptuously) in the beginnings of what will no doubt become a prostitution racket as the James Bay Development Corporation continues to "open a fascinating vista" for the Indian people of James Bay.

3 0020 00357 1041

Few of the Indians in the area are against development
and change: they have lived with change all their lives,
and expect it. But they are solidly against the James Bay
project, because of its brutal assault on nature, its certain destruction of the country food to which they attach
so strong a spiritual value, and its destruction of every
Indian value that has been handed down to them
through the generations.